T0248139

CRYBABY

Also by Donna-Claire Chesman

The Book of Mac: Remembering Mac Miller

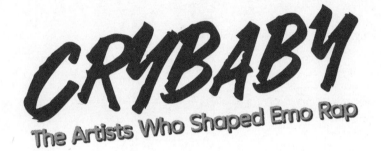

CRYBABY
The Artists Who Shaped Emo Rap

DONNA-CLAIRE
CHESMAN

PERMUTED
PRESS

A PERMUTED PRESS BOOK

Crybaby:
The Artists Who Shaped Emo Rap
© 2025 by Donna-Claire Chesman
All Rights Reserved

ISBN: 978-1-63758-802-4
ISBN (eBook): 978-1-63758-803-1

Cover art by Jim Villaflores
Cover image by Adreeonah Toro
Interior design and composition by Greg Johnson, Textbook Perfect

This is a work of nonfiction. All people, locations, events, and situations are portrayed to the best of the author's memory.

PERMUTED
PRESS

Permuted Press, LLC
New York • Nashville
permutedpress.com

Published in the United States of America
1 2 3 4 5 6 7 8 9 10

For every generation of crybabies.

Contents

What Is Emo Rap?

Sean "Slug" Daley (rapper, Atmosphere): I invented the term "emo rap" in, like, 1998 in an interview for *URB*. It was an interview about Deep Puddle Dynamics, and someone paid a publicist and we got a piece in *URB*, written by Dave Thompkins, and he was asking the four of us random questions and made the piece a collage of our answers. He asked me to describe what our style of rap sounds like, and I said: "Cynical, minimalistic, emo rap." That's what I do, and that's what I bring to the table.

Then, I started using the phrase *a lot*. I worked in record stores and all the emo, we were just putting it in punk. Sunny Day Real Estate would go into punk. So, to me, "emo rap" was funny. It ended up sticking! I lived to regret it, because it became a way to disparage us. People started using it as a way to belittle us—almost like, "That's not real hip-hop, that's *emo rap*."

Tom Breihan (author, senior editor, *Stereogum*): I honestly don't know what emo rap *is*. I'm not sure it can be counted as a genre, necessarily. It's a term I've shied away from using—all rap music is emotional, even if it's the most cold, calculating music. There is emotion behind that. As far as I know, the thing that came to be known as emo rap is part of an outgrowth of late '90s, early 2000s, where

1

just as straight-up emo, none of the people wanted that genre to be applied to them.

Cat Zhang (music critic): For me, it's associated with a kind of pessimistic worldview—Juice WRLD comes to mind.

Taz Taylor (Internet Money founder and producer): It's the content. If it's really emotional and people are talking about their problems—I don't know how to explain it. It's that 2000s pop-punk shit. The beats and music get updated. We combine rap with pop-punk and that's what it is. Same content they was talking about [in the 2000s]. It comes down to lyrics, ultimately. If I give someone a guitar, it doesn't mean they're making an emo song.

Ivie Ani (journalist, cultural critic, and on-air correspondent): I look at emo rap as this subgenre of hip-hop that is fused with rock music. Millennials are more familiar with that emo rock music era of the early 2000s, and emo rap came about in the mid-2010s and the proliferation of SoundCloud. As far as content, emo rap is about young people expressing themselves and talking about heavy themes: depression, drug use, loneliness, nihilism, even suicide. But, I would venture that there's always been some semblance of that type of rap, since the beginning of hip-hop. These elements existed in hip-hop before the emo genre existed.

Matthew Strauss (music critic): Singing about self-deprecation and worse at times: self-harm. Auto-Tuned, melodic singing, in rap parlance, with a rap beat—although that's not so necessary.

A-Trak (DJ, president of Fool's Gold Records): Emo rap mainly has melodies that were inspired by a certain era of emo rock. There were certainly other attributes: a certain vulnerability and subject matter. But for me, it's the melodies first. I was never really into the emo rock groups that inspired this, so these sensibilities aren't really my thing in the first place, but I got used to that coming into the language of hip-hop.

Colin Joyce (music critic): There are a couple different definitions. One is: there's no such thing as emo rap. The other is: all rap is emo rap. I'm not sure which I believe more! The genre the term refers to is a SoundCloud development in the mid-2010s, but I see it as a pretty linear development of a lot of stuff that is built into rap from inception. A lot of rap is about pain and bringing out that emotional expression in ways that feel fresh and new. People talk about the use of samples and mall-goth guitars. In a broad sense, I think of the term as a continuation of what's always happened in rap, and more specifically: rappers on SoundCloud in the 2010s.

Emma Garland (music critic): Emo always seems to be attached to genres that are more traditionally masculine. It originally came as a descriptor on the back of hardcore, and then there were bands articulating themselves in a more "feminine" way: higher pitched vocals, sensitive lyrics, and the delivery was sort of "hysterical." I think it's the same with emo rap as well. The stylistic choices and the way people articulate themselves feels feminine, in a traditional sense, to the mass audience. On a more blatant level, it's rappers who have been raised on noughties emo, and then mashed those sensibilities together.

Paul Thompson (music critic): It has to either be first-person, or be the kind of writing that is nominally a third-person thing, but everyone knows you're writing about a girl or something. It has to feel diaristic. You have to feel, as the listener, as if you are entering into some sort of intimate exchange with the artist, where they are revealing something and hoping to connect with you. Of course, this is a type of posturing, but it scans differently from the type of posturing of, "I'm the better MC than you."

Hanif Abdurraqib (author, *A Little Devil in America*): So often, emo as a genre or aesthetic, is something that hinges on emotional sensitivity that is usually expressed through straight men. It had less to do with a sound, and more to do with the impulse to define or put emotions in a box. For me, there's been emotional sensitivity in rap for as long as I've listened to rap. I don't know if there are folks who are *specialists*. LL Cool J, at one point, was perhaps an early adopter of the benefits reaped by exuberant expression of emotions.

midwxst (rapper): Emo rap is a subgenre of hip-hop where a lot of the topics are very, very personal. You listen to it if you want to relate to what somebody's going through. You could throw on a song by an emo rapper, and that song would hit different for you—if you're going through something, it could be a comfort. You can relate to what you're listening to! Not a lot of artists can explain the feeling of being alone. It's very vulnerable.

Pranav Trewn (music critic): There's the strict literalism of emotional rap, which plenty of rap is emotional. Geto Boys, Biggie. There's plenty of emotion and talk of mental health. Then, on the flip side, there's the stereotype of emo rap, that's the Juice WRLDs of the world. Something closer to pop punk, and in the most negative light, the immature outburst of emotion. I would include both of those pillars in my definition, and Kid Cudi is the clearest embodiment of the, "You'll know it when you hear it" in emo rap. The definition really comes down to personal struggle as the guiding light of their work. There's rap that seeks to empower, and emo rap is about meeting you where you are a little more closely.

Intro: 2017

I'M SHIVERING ON A RIVERSIDE PARK BENCH IN NEW JERSEY. SPRING hasn't quite taken hold. There's snow on the green landing, and the water seen from the lookout point is more a series of frozen ribbons. I turn to my buddy—one day, many years from now, he'll be the best man at my wedding—and he shows me his phone.

"Have you heard of Lil Peep?" he asks.

YouTube is loaded up and the video for a song called "witchblades" plays on mute. It's like being offered a rare curio. In the video, Peep and Lil Tracy dance in an alley and in a cramped bedroom. It's lo-fi. There's flashes of thin chains, and brown liquor, and switchblades. They look like they're having a blast. My buddy clicks the sound up and what I hear is transfixing. Dramatic piano notes match right up to Peep's chanting, "switchblades, cocaine." The production is slight—just the essentials of a bottomed-out bass line and skittering claps to accompany the melody, if you can call it that. My buddy watches me watch in silence, unaware my brain is being terraformed.

The song ends. My buddy says, certainly, that this music makes no sense and why does anyone listen to this stuff anyway? It's a good question, but not for the reasons he thinks. I ask him where he found Peep, and he tells me his songs are big on SoundCloud. That makes sense. We get food and drinks and part ways for the night. I tuck into bed hours later, and search up Lil Peep on my phone. I find a mixtape called *cry-baby*. I queue it up and hear a tender roll call for a generation: "she says I'm a crybaby...." And it's not that it clicks instantly, but it hooks into my skin. I try to avoid the itch, even try to consider the music kind of lame, but I keep coming back. Eventually, I listen to *crybaby* every night for a month.

One night, splayed out in my bed with nowhere to go and nothing to do, I find "star shopping" and I well up in tears at the track's desperation. "Can I get one conversation at least?" is the backbone of a hymn. The sparse guitar strumming and dejected singing leaves enough room for a personal narrative to emerge. I remember every breakup at once. They flatten me and I cry some more, and I listen to the song again. It's a tipped dart—I never stood a chance. Things start to connect from there. I open myself up to the idea that Lil Peep might just be the voice of a lonely generation.

Summer hits, and the video for "Awful Things" comes out in August. This power-pop-meets-emo-rap ballad, this *thing*, confirms for me that Lil Peep is about to be the biggest artist alive. His youthful whispers have matured into arena-sized howls. "Bother me / Tell me awful things" is a Madison Square Garden–sized emotion born from a bedroom genre. The video, set in a high school where Peep is a delinquent loverboy meeting his crush in a crusty, strobing bathroom, ends with Peep setting himself and the whole school on fire. He stands center-frame, in a heartbroken inferno, ready to fall in love all over again. The video and song are just a hair over three minutes—I am convinced this is the pinnacle of rap cinema.

In November, when Lil Peep's death first breaks one night on Twitter, I stay up all night refreshing my feed and waiting for an official source to confirm the clout-chasing gossip blogs are all wrong. It never comes. Too stunned to cry, I will myself to sleep. The next morning, I loop up "Save That Shit" as a companion for a cold morning walk. I angrily mutter some lyrics to myself: "nothing like them other motherfuckers, I can make you rich." Despite my insistence, he doesn't come back to life. When I realize Peep's death is permanent, it swallows me up and the tears come as I'm standing on the sidewalk. The chill cuts my face. The more I sob, the more the oncoming winter wind grates my skin. All the while I have "Fuck my life, can't save that, girl" blaring through my earbuds. I think of the cord connecting me to my iPod as an IV.

The thing about emo rap is that it's *my* music. It's a massive sigh of relief. When Lil Peep's songs first flooded my veins, I had no idea the genre would become a focal point of my tastes and obsessions. This stuff was whiny, base, and *quiet*. Those early Peep singles had no pomp. They were disarming and meek, yet the emotions were elemental. They consumed me. To this day, I see flashes of my ugliest memories in *crybaby*, and I feel less alone. And that's the point of emo, right? To be your friend when you don't really know how to make any, and to help you feel better when being alive feels like wearing hand-me-down clothes.

Atmosphere Gives Emo Rap
Its Name

Slug: When I was making *God Loves Ugly*, I was starting to realize there might just be a job here. Prior, I didn't have any hopes that this was gonna translate into a career. I was hobby-rapping because people were letting me. The money that was coming in was enough to support the habit and to keep rapping—none of us were paying our bills. Myself, Ant, Musab, Saddiq, we all worked side jobs. Saddiq and me had just opened up a record store, and were trying to figure out how to make *that* work, while working side jobs, while writing.

We did a tour off *Lucy Ford*, while I was making *God Loves Ugly*. That tour brought in some money to supplement our incomes. That's when we thought we had something. I might have cracked a certain code. It was me, J-Bird, Eyedea, Abilities. I went out every night, mingling and mixing, meeting everyone and going to all the radio stations. I was going to all the record stores, trying to meet people. I *enjoyed* it. Here I was, one step closer to all these things I loved as a kid. It was bringing me closer to people who were doing all these things I wanted to do.

All of that friendliness translated into people buying my tapes and supporting us, and playing my tapes on their radio shows. *Woah!*

Okay.... We weren't really in the industry yet. I was just starting to toy with the idea of publicity. I was touring the *Lucy Ford* stuff when I met Kathryn Frazier from Biz 3. People who were in the industry way further than me—I liked who they were and what they were doing. I was just making friends.

While I'm doing this, on my off-time I'm recording the songs with Ant that would become *God Loves Ugly*. All of these songs were informed by the people we met while touring. Some of these people responded to the *Lucy Ford* stuff. "Wow, you're talking about being insecure, but also are confident at the same time?" I was just nodding like a bobble-head. I didn't know I was putting that into *Lucy Ford*. I was just writing what I felt.

Here I am getting confidence boosts but also getting shit on by some of my peers for making more emo-style rap. I had defensive reactions to getting shit on—and to receiving compliments. I was touring, I was trying to wrap my head around what I was, and I was a lost *dad*. I was on the road, missing my kid at home, even though I was a part-time dad. This was all very confusing as a twenty-eight-year-old. In my mind, what was expected of me was to have a full-time job, mortgage, and some insurance for the kid. I did not have *any* of that. I barely finished high school.

Hitting the road and seeing these places that were not like where I was from—New York, versus Memphis, versus Alabama. It was a lot for me to take in, while also missing what I thought I was supposed to become. I didn't see any of this in me in real-time. This is all hindsight. All of that went into what I was writing on *God Loves Ugly*. That is the difference between *God Loves Ugly* and *Overcast! Overcast!* was very short-sighted. When I made *God Loves Ugly*, I had experiences outside of my city, outside of my country. It made me realize how special Minneapolis was. I grew up as a small kid who saw the world as a giant, scary place. I realized I'm actually a big kid, and the world is small. That informed *God Loves Ugly*. That's why you can hear me go from insecure to overconfident. It all was true.

I'll tell you what, the boogeyman at twenty-eight, thirty-eight, forty-eight, forty-nine, where I am now, it's being alone. It's the idea of, I'm gonna die at some point and when I do, I don't want to die how my father died. He was by himself. When the EMTs arrived, he was already gone. He called 911, but by the time they got there, he didn't make it. It was just his cats. That's the fear. Still, to this day—I don't mean to cry....

I had this partner, and even though the two of us never wanted to compromise and make life easier for each other, because we were both very stubborn, she taught me a lot about what I was, and who I could be. I had a great mom, too, who instilled a lot of great shit in me. But watching my partner, in real-time, put everybody before herself, that really gave me a lot of insight into how to approach life. We were sleeping in people's apartments after shows, so being able to make sure everybody I was surrounded by, if I couldn't take care of them, at least make sure they feel good.

I was surrounded by opportunists, and I decided to become the opposite. *God Loves Ugly* was informed by keeping myself open to learning from people about how to *be*. A lot of times, we teach young artists to be opportunists, and I wonder if that's the way. When we toured *God Loves Ugly*, I realized there was a magnet inside of me that drew me to good people, and drew the good people to me. That was the era of my life where I could've went off the rails. I could've been a really sad story. One of the stories you tell to scare young artists. But there was a magnet in me that drew me to a different kind of person. A person who wanted to be a part of the sum, as opposed to a sum of the parts. For me to encounter that at thirty and realize that's the way I wanted to go…that's the universe working. If things had lined up for me at twenty-two, I would've been a bad story.

I was considering the long game, considering what I wanted to be for my son. Even when I was in Minneapolis during *God Loves Ugly*, I was crashing on couches. I wasn't nomadic—that's too poetic. I had money in my pocket to stay in a hotel, but I wasn't ready to figure out where or how I wanted to live. That record dropped, we started touring, and I went into this pocket of booze, loneliness, and trying to cure that loneliness with booze. I threw a lot of myself into random companionship because I just wanted to sit next to someone.

There was definitely an angel over me, keeping me safe through all that. It wasn't that long of a stint, either. People who listen to our music have a romanticized idea of what this was for me. But when I look at how long it lasted, compared to how long my career has lasted, it was a smaller portion. By the time I lost my hair, I was like, "Yo, I gotta start taking care of myself." It's interesting for me to sit here and think about it, but *God Loves Ugly* was the height of being fueled by insecurity. I was just a loose meteor floating through the galaxy. Definitely there was a destination I was heading for. I don't think I ever thought, *I'm gonna crash.*

* * *

A CHORUS OF CHILDREN CHANTING, "YOU'RE SO UGLY." SCARS, toxicity, and dysfunctional relationships with women. Self-hatred galore. These are the flourishes that define rap duo Atmosphere's *God Loves Ugly*, the album that helped codify emo rap. Released on Rhymesayers Entertainment in June 2002, this was the waxy seal of potential for a genre named mostly in jest. *God Loves Ugly* took the intense self-deprecation of emo rock, soaked it in cheap beer and self-loathing, and wrung it out across a series of singular hip-hop productions.

"Back when I made *God Loves Ugly*, I was just making what *I* made," Atmosphere's rapper Slug tells me a few weeks after the album's twentieth anniversary. "I was doing my best to make something that felt right and honest to me, that felt like I wasn't being fake. I wanted to be genuine. I'm projecting who I want to be into my art. At the same time, I can't over-project. I have to be genuine."

By the time *God Loves Ugly* came out, Atmosphere had landed finally on the match of Sean "Slug" Daley and DJ-producer Anthony "Ant" Davis. Coming up on the underground indie scene in Minneapolis, the first proper Atmosphere album, 1997's *Overcast!*, was a series of narrative exercises. Rigorous touring helped Atmosphere become one of the faces of the Midwest underground rap scene. "Slug wasn't just rapping about his emotions," says author and *Stereogum* senior editor Tom Breihan. "He was rapping about his own inadequacy and his dysfunctional relationships. That's the stuff the emo bands of this time were talking about—he was touring the same venues of those bands. He existed in this quasi-indie-rock context."

Atmosphere's swerve towards emo rap began at the turn of the century with the *Lucy Ford: The Atmosphere EPs*. These acetic songs hooked into the underground scene of Minneapolis, and kicked off the touring machine that still fuels Atmosphere to this day, but they weren't as transfixing as the first-person revelations that would come in *God Loves Ugly*.

"I was trying to do what my heroes had done," Slug explains. "I made a bunch of songs that people may not have heard somebody else speak to in that way." Influenced deeply by Geto Boys' Scarface, Slug set out to write from a tortured perspective. *God Loves Ugly* is explicit, id-driven, and unnerving, forming a mold for an entire subgenre. The first play of "Fuck You Lucy" codified the whole scene: "Most of this garbage I write that these people seem to like / Is about you and how I let you infect my life." It's the type of ex-hating screed that was nurtured by emo rock, refashioned into a wounded dispatch from the Minnesota hip-hop underground. Slug had to be a more-than-competent emcee to get by. Instant skeptics could not be won over by raw emotionality alone. Conviction is the heart of this album. If the self-hate didn't sound as impassioned and genuine as it did, *God Loves Ugly* would not have come to define any genre. It would have been a whisper.

Instead, Slug's sharp accounts of his abject failure to be a decent human being allowed him to open a door for a generation of rap artists to shine a light on the lamer aspects of their lives. In 2002, Slug was rapping with a zeal that would suggest his life was on the line, while lashing himself in the process. His approach differed from the anguish of the previous generation's stars: The Notorious B.I.G.'s "Suicidal Thoughts" is as pained as any emo rap highlight, but the late Biggie doesn't invite the same personal takedown we see blossoming with Atmosphere. Biggie was an unwavering titan; Slug was a heap of insecurities.

God Loves Ugly takes place at the bottom of a ravine littered with the rubble of a shattered man. "I look at Scarface or Mobb Deep—they talked about the dark sides of their brains. That's my version of emo," Slug says. "When I was doing that, I wasn't reinventing the wheel. I didn't create nothing new, but I gave it a name. It's more than, 'I feel like this,' it's, 'How do your feelings affect your surroundings?' I didn't know that's what I was writing at the time. I looked at how my generational and childhood traumas affected me, and how I impacted myself. I rapped about it."

On these early Atmosphere records, there was no line not worth crossing. It helps that Ant provides the perfect playground for Slug. Singles "GodLovesUgly" and "Modern Man's Hustle" represented two pieces of the Atmosphere promise: relatability and pop parlance. Here is a needling album, a near-elegant car crash from which you can't look away—one that makes you feel like it could be you in that driver's seat. The way Slug writes about his failures, the way he lights himself on fire from song to song, is novel because of just how far he goes in on *himself*. These songs are gushing lacerations laid to wax with little shame.

"When I listen to that record, I have those physical reactions to remembering who I was and where I was when I made it," Slug says.

On *God Loves Ugly*, Slug exists in a rich hip-hop lineage. The album was arresting on impact, with curious critics using Slug's music as a vehicle to bring up tired readings of rap as unfeeling until this very moment in time. These writers were just shy of the larger point. Slug's personal irreverence ultimately helped him transcend and make emo rap into something less amorphous and more identifiable. "I don't want to overstate the novelty of rappers rapping about emo things, about their feelings," says music critic Paul Thompson. "But what I would term emo rap—and I'm biased because I grew up in the Twin Cities—it is that turn-of-the-century Rhymesayers stuff. That type of personal, psychologically tortured music dates back to, and before, the early Scarface and Geto Boys stuff. In terms of a specific subgenre, I go to Rhymesayers first."

Midwest staple Rhymesayers Entertainment was founded in 1995 by Slug, Musab "Sab the Artist" Sadd, and Brent "Siddiq" Sayers. The label arrived on the heels of the dissolution of the underground rap crew Headshots and has gone on to be a beacon of independent hip-hop—and a home for emo rap's earliest pioneers to thrive. "We're the little engine that could," Slug said of the label in a 2015 *Forbes* interview[1] celebrating twenty years of RSE. In addition to Atmosphere, in the early days, the label was home to a handful of critical acts from Minnesota, including duo Eyedea & Abilities, whose 2001 album *First Born* is an underground gem and a clear precursor to the dour flavor of *God Loves Ugly*.

First Born has a dense and literary quality, with the late Eyedea's battle rap past coloring his deliveries. It feels like the high-minded emo of the nineties, particularly the early Jawbreaker records, which are so tightly coiled. Eyedea unspools a knotty personal philosophy across an hour of songs, laying groundwork for Slug to go even further, even more divergent, and deliver *God Loves Ugly*'s self-aimed critiques. Rhymesayers was becoming known for headier than heady bar maelstroms: at one point on *First Born*, Eyedea says, "This is the consciousness revolution," which isn't all that uncommon considering how much of rap was and continues to be focused on opening the third eye. Slug's work helped to personalize the label's offerings. Where Eyedea appeared as the brains, Atmosphere remains the bleeding heart.

These days, Slug compares relistening to *God Loves Ugly* to shuddering, as if he's noticing all the trauma he's been carrying in his body. This may be the closest Slug will get to experiencing the intensity of his earlier music from the perspective of a fan in need. "There's a lot of fans that take just the parts that feel bad so they can drink, listen, and feel bad," he recounts. Had he made the album today, he "would've definitely deposited some gems of looking into therapy, instead of it being so insular."

Yet the myopic focus is a massive reason why the album landed and catalyzed emo. *God Loves Ugly* deals in tension; the album's logic would fall apart if Slug included an interlude about seeking help. Not that the music suggests he was in any position to do so. Instead, *God Loves Ugly* uses snippets of dialogue from women who have been antagonized by Slug's shitty behavior—a project of his own insecurities. "A Song About A Friend" begins with a woman telling Slug he's a "fucking freak," and him replying, "What do you mean, freak?" The introduction to "Hair" features similar deprecation, with Slug playing up his own inadequacies. It's all very desperate, and it works.

"We made 'Hair,' originally, to much darker music," Slug recalls. "The music Ant gave me was almost haunting—like a horror film. It was one of the first times we tried to incorporate a live instrument. The song itself was harsh. Same lyrics! It was just *harsh*. It was a throwaway. We probably made forty songs for *God Loves Ugly*. Over half of the songs we demoed got thrown away. Then, Ant was like, 'Why don't we try ["Hair"] over this and say the words in a more fun way.' Immediately, the jokes were showing themselves.

"We didn't know how it would work—there's nothing very *fun* about the album. Back then, I used to carry a camcorder around with me. We were playing a show in New York, and we were working the *Lucy Ford* stuff. We didn't have much of a set. MF DOOM was playing that night. Outside, after the show, some girls were talking and they were a little drunk and I was like, 'Hey, say something cool,' and she said the shit at the beginning of 'Hair.' She gave this goofy song an intro, and I didn't even know it at the time! I had that before we made the song. I found the soundbyte and, 'Oh, my God! We can put this on the song.' Now the song works."

"Hair" hinged on an intro that was overwhelmingly a negative read of Atmosphere's cool. Elsewhere, the question of whether Atmosphere, or just Slug himself, was appealing in any way was constantly interrogated. These brief exchanges were emo in their own way based on how borderline goofy they were, but also self-serious. It boasted the "musical and thematic urgency" Andy Greenwald teased out in his critical work on emo rock, *Nothing Feels Good*.[2] The same summer Atmosphere released *God Loves Ugly*, Greenwald pointed out that emo band Saves The Day was playing Madison Square Garden in New York City. "Emo has broken in America," Greenwald wrote. "The sensitivity, hooks, and average-guy appeal" of emo rock had its fingerprints all over *God Loves Ugly*.

"Slug was rapping about being a dirtbag and a loser in ways that were not new to rap, but were unconventional," Breihan explains. "Most rap music is about imposing your will on a hostile environment and rising up. Slug's whole thing was more about 'Our environment isn't necessarily hostile, we're just dudes.... We're not gonna try to rise up and transcend.' It was all about getting lost in your own identity as a scumbag."

Seediness is baked into Slug's approach to writing. This stuff is, at its core, distasteful. It harkens back to the way all punk is an expression of being, in some way or another, gross. "For Atmosphere, that self-deprecation was a big, big thing," Breihan affirms. "Atmosphere's thing was 'I'm shittier than you; I'm grosser than you.'"

A needle-drop test of this album reveals as much. Be it the way each song approaches women—"A place for men to express heartbreak doesn't mean all those songs have evolved views of women," Thompson agrees—or the grimy content of "stepping in my cum" that Slug raps about on "The Bass And The Movement." Or any number of lines, verses, choruses, and bridges. The album is solid, but it is held together by scorned, dark bands and tar from tobacco.

And yet it is also wildly accessible. Slug's lack of posturing, and his obviously hurt feelings, invites a certain gaze unto the record—one that pities him for being *him*. This positioning of Slug as an unfortunately lovable anti-hero colors emo rap for the next two decades. Newer artists following Slug's canon over the years—Kid Cudi, 6 Dogs, Yung Lean, Lil Peep—used an outcast persona to draw listeners in. Equally exhausting and honest, the outright cringe of *God Loves Ugly* was foundational.

"There's a lot of cringey shit on those old records," Slug says. "Back then, the cringe was gross. Nowadays, the cringe is corny. But that's always been part of *me*. Cringe or not, I'm gonna go for it. It's always been a risk I've been willing to take. I didn't turn off Slug to be Sean. They're the same person, but it was very self-aware because I'm a dad, or my mom is paying attention. So with those gross things, you'd always hear me either joking or saying it for a reason. There are some lines that I wish I could erase, because they were ignorant."

It would be disingenuous to write about *God Loves Ugly* without mentioning the hope peering through the darkness. There is a survivor's instinct permeating the album. For as miserable as Slug appears on wax, there is such a bombast to his voice, it's hard to imagine him doing anything other than getting through. He accomplishes this dance best on "Lovelife," where he raps, "Here I am, thinking about death again / Humbles out the stress, helps the breath get in" before getting to the meat of the track. The hook of "Lovelife" is a wrestling match between angels and demons, culminating in Slug's proverbial freedom once he's six feet under. The ending chants of "Love / Life" are haunting. They are Slug struggling against the straps of self-loathing.

This highwire act prevents *God Loves Ugly* from falling flat with retread themes. The strongest practitioners of the genre bring a definitive sense of personality and perspective to otherwise basic tropes of heartache and women-hating. "The people who reject emo rap, they see it as so forgiving, but I don't," Thompson explains. "You are trafficking in personal revelations, those have to be *interesting*. You can't skate on style that much, and there's only so many human experiences. You're setting out to write a song on heartbreak that's uniquely interesting, when that's a huge percentage of the history of recorded music. It's hard!"

On *God Loves Ugly*, Slug was up to the challenge of originality. His writing makes the album stick to the ribs all these years later. The incisive nature of Slug's first-person accounts helped to turn *God Loves Ugly* from underground darling into a classic. In June 2022, Tom Breihan covered the album in a twentieth-anniversary piece for *Stereogum*[3] and was just as taken with Slug's work: "Much of the credit for *God Loves Ugly* belongs to Slug, a gifted writer who rapped charismatically about his lack of charisma and who carried conviction in his voice even when describing crippling dysfunction."

"It was a very, very good rap album that came out as a product of this underground that was just bubbling at the time," Breihan tells me a few weeks after the piece was published. "This was Scribble Jam, after Eminem's fame, and Atmosphere came from that context of Midwestern underground. They connected with scenes elsewhere—they had El-P on *Lucy Ford*, and they had connections with MURS and all that. So this was an underground scene that people who liked indie rock could recognize, because it had the same sort of ethos."

God Loves Ugly endures because of Slug's intensity and sincerity. One of the first lines on the record basks in dirtbag insecurity—"Maybe you don't like us," which is followed a few songs later by sampling the lyric "she still wonders why I'm so insecure"—and yet this record is not inherently off-putting. Slug's diaristic approach to writing and his unquantifiable, uncanny charisma makes the album welcoming. It's that "Ah, finally!" moment for droves of fans who evidently saw themselves in the rapper's countless failings. This was rap music for losers who wanted to feel at least a little built up before the inevitable fall. That, too, makes this record so emo. The album gives listeners the sense they're holding something precious, just for them, and it helps build a lifelong relationship between them and Atmosphere. Here, emo rap becomes just as much about the music, as it is about the connection the listener develops to the art and the artist.

"It's crazy to me that *God Loves Ugly* is the one," Slug remarks. "It was recorded on an eight-track. The sounds are just really—it almost sounds like something your friends made. If you put it next to other albums in 2002, it does not sound as full or big. It's lo-fi, not that we were trying to make something lo-fi. We were making something as hi-fi as we could. There's an aesthetic there that is attractive.

"A lot of *God Loves Ugly*, you're hearing the version of the song we gave birth to. We just handed you the baby. The writing on that album captured me in my late twenties. It would speak to people, if they're in the right part of their life, there's something that gets captured in that record that we didn't capture in any other of our albums. It's a confusion and a searching, trying to figure out *something*. That's a common thing that goes across genders, races...that feeling of trying to figure out your shit before you die. That speaks to people."

Good emo rap does not attempt to be groundbreaking. These are not new stories—they never will be. The most effective emo rap, the enduring stuff, is the most sincere and often lamest version of an act. When an artist sets out to write a song, and they discover something unexpected and scary in themselves, and then share that with the listener, that's the spark. When the listener sinks into an Atmosphere song for the first or fiftieth time and is startled by what they see in themselves, that's the magic. Emo rap does not obscure the performing artist—it doesn't ride away on the angst of "I'm so sad right now," ignoring any other substance—fundamentally, it is a revelatory genre. It makes the artist and the listener ask pertinent and challenging questions, consciously or otherwise. It unveils the ugliest parts of people for the—we hope—greater good.

"We play shows and there's sixteen-year-olds and fifty-six-year-olds out there," Slug says. "I'm looking at younger people like, *What the fuck are you here for?* I get it, this is speaking to them. They're *hearing* it."

Within connection is commercial appeal, however small in comparison to what emo rap would become by the late 2010s. "There are a lot of songs on *God Loves Ugly* that have different approaches, and they're all potential hits," Thompson says. "They're the college radio, club circuit level of hit, and they're all pretty emo." Breihan opens his anniversary piece with a similar sentiment: "Once upon a time, I fucked around and convinced myself that 'The Bass And The Movement,' the second song on Atmosphere's album *God Loves Ugly*, could be a hit." Both of these points identify the potential for emo rap to reach critical mass, though it wouldn't truly happen until 2017 when Lil Uzi Vert's "XO Tour Llif3" hit the Billboard Hot 100 and got people dancing to a suicidal smash.

In 2018, the *Chicago Reader*'s Leor Galil penned "How Atmosphere accidentally predicted Juice Wrld."[4] The headline speaks for itself, capturing the way music evolves and how the shouts of one become the cries of many: "The new class of emo rappers—the ones who also get called Soundcloud rappers—actually make music that owes a debt to Atmosphere, whether they know it or not."

"My music, Scarface's music, and Juice WRLD's music...all three of us, you could trace it back to people caught up in a cycle of self-medicating," Slug explains when I ask him about the article. "It's just people trying to figure out how to feel okay in this world. I have a feeling Juice

WRLD never heard an Atmosphere song in his life—and I wouldn't fault him for that! I don't think we're connected to Juice WRLD in any way other than how people chose to *use* our music."

The impact of an Atmosphere record, or a hit from the late Juice WRLD, then, must be the same. Whether you're wallowing in cheap booze or in the whir of a ceiling fan that soundtracks the suburban bedroom malaise, or some in-between point that feels just as destructive, people scream Juice WRLD lyrics for the same reason they nod along to Atmosphere songs: it feels *right*.

"For around fifteen years now, 'emo rap' has been applied to a long string of artists, many of them radically different from one another," Galil wrote. "But the unwitting early-2000s originators of the subgenre and today's Lil Xans and Lil Peeps have a few things in common: They've all made music that exposes surprising vulnerability, they've all borrowed from punk aesthetics, and they've all launched their careers underground, sometimes in reaction to mainstream hip-hop trends."

Galil's 2018 assessment of emo rap echoes a key point Jon Caramanica hit on in 2004, something that would resonate with emo rap artists and fans—at least in the early days of their success, before the majors got involved and streaming took hold of music distribution—for the next twenty years: "The career path of these artists is decidedly punk: low-budget albums, self-booked tours."

Speaking with music writer Danielle Chelosky, Caramanica's sentiments continue to ring true: "Lil Peep came up through Gothboiclique, which is a DIY music collective, which is so punk! Also, the way Peep behaved with all his friends, and trying to bring them up with him—that is so sincere. Juice WRLD also started off independent. That's why they're considered emo, and that matters."

Still, the sound of an Atmosphere record has little to do with Juice WRLD and Lil Peep's gothic piano and blaring guitar, their emphasis on melody and the ever-important wail. Emo rap was codified with *God Loves Ugly*, but that does not make the definition any more immediate to a casual or seasoned listener. Emo rap remains nebulous, narrowed down by the proverbial moment you puke after being punched in the gut. "Emo has blown up and become this whole other beast now, but all music is emotional," Breihan says. "I find [emo rap] to be a term of limited usefulness that now seems to cover less of an aesthetic thing, but more of a culture. There is an emo universe."

Within the universe of emo Breihan identifies, there is the supplemental question of how this music is being received by those who need it most. The people who struggle with depression or substance abuse—are they hearing *God Loves Ugly* and finding validation in Slug, or a cautionary tale? As the originator of emo rap as we know it, Slug finds a need to divorce himself from a majority of *God Loves Ugly*, for his own sake. "I don't think the music is a hall pass to get blackout drunk," he reflects. "But more so, when they are getting drunk, they play this record. To me, that creates a bond between this music and that behavior. When they break that pattern of behavior, what happens to the music? I know what it means to me: I have left that album behind. All the songs I still perform at shows, I choose them intentionally. I am not performing them from the space of who I was twenty years ago."

Whether Slug's estimations are correct, whether the record gives license to listeners to make bad decisions, his ability to reflect on a twenty-year-old album is rare within a genre ravaged by drug-related deaths, untimely passings, and gun violence. Emo rap artists largely do not get the opportunity to speak from a mature perspective on their work. There is no chance to reflect for Lil Peep, Juice WRLD, 6 Dogs, and XXXTentacion. These artists do not get the privilege of growing up and growing out of their work as Slug has, and perhaps that makes their music even more precious within the context of how raw and ultimately unformed the releases are. There is a sense, when listening to late artists' catalogs, listeners stand at a threshold that has been bricked off by circumstance. It hurts not to know what's next, but we can at least relish in where this music came from.

Kid Cudi's "Day 'N' Nite" Introduces Sensitivity to Emo Rap

THE LATE 2000S SAW EMO RAP TRANSITION FROM THE UNDER-ground grime of hip-hop duo Atmosphere into something more syrupy and tender, marked most clearly by the commercial debut single and subsequent mixtape from Scott "Kid Cudi" Mescudi. The Ohio native's global smash "Day 'N' Nite," produced by Cudi's longtime friend Dot Da Genius, was first uploaded to MySpace in 2007. By early 2008, after receiving a wider push and a bevy of remixes on award-winning DJ A-Trak's label Fool's Gold, the Grammy-nominated single changed the course of emo rap.

"My first experience with that song was very primal and simple," A-Trak recalls. "I knew Plain Pat from my work with Kanye, and Pat hit me one day and wanted to play me two or three records from some new rapper. He sent me 'Day 'N' Nite.' Pat was working at Def Jam, but there was this implied statement of, 'Major labels aren't going to understand this yet. Should we try something on Fool's Gold?' I went on a trip to Australia. A few days after Pat had sent me the songs, I ended up listening to 'Day 'N' Nite' for hours and hours and hours on that flight. I remember thinking, *We have to do something with this song. I can't stop listening to it*. It was hypnotic. I remember Pat and I having a conversation about the beat itself sounding a little unpolished. I was just vaguely aware that Cudi and his friend made the track themselves. We decided to leave it as-is."

"Day 'N' Nite" was the byproduct of Cudi moving to New York in hopes of launching a rap career and immediately facing emotional and financial hardships. Cudi lived with his uncle for a time, but their relationship ended on poor terms, and his uncle passed away in 2006 before they could reconcile. As Cudi told *Complex* in 2009, the final state of their relationship ate him up inside.[1] "Day 'N' Nite" was written in response to a swell of lingering regret and drew inspiration from the seminal Geto Boys track, "Mind Playing Tricks on Me." Completed in a matter of days, the song peaked at No. 3 on the *Billboard* Hot 100. It was a mighty turning point in pop culture.

Cudi introduced the idea of an emo rapper that could be your best friend from up the block. The accessibility of Kid Cudi's suffering allowed hordes of people trapped in their bedrooms to see themselves one-to-one with the artist. Grafting yourself onto a Cudi narrative was easier than the hyper-specific screeds Atmosphere delivered. On wax, Cudi sounded alienated from his struggles, as though he'd already drowned and washed ashore. The trauma had moved through his body, and now he could report from the gallows of his soft despair. Such a measure of distance helped open up emo rap to a wider audience.

Cudi's writing was only gently tortured. Though it dealt with complex feelings of loss and isolation, it was extremely approachable. Cudi was friendly in his delivery—there was a late-night-at-the-kitchen-table-with-friends energy to the single. And as it so happens, "Day 'N' Nite" would go on to soundtrack rambling, existentially anxious evenings for listeners the world over. The song scanned as trustworthy, having the essential quality of providing much needed companionship to its audience.

"In the 2000s in general there was a shift of the typical rapper persona," A-Trak says. "The Pharrells, Kanyes, and Lupes made it cool to be a nerd and punctured the myth of the macho rapper. But Cudi, even with his style of dressing, he took all that further to where it wasn't just a question of the rapper being a tough guy. They could be very, very vulnerable, and bring in themes of depression." Tinges of psychological pain were already a mainstay in rap music, but the way Cudi was able to popify the content—without making it childish, or worse, insincere—gave the growing mental health conversation in hip-hop and popular culture an even stronger foundation.

By the late 2000s, the shape of angst had changed. The world was slowly falling into a new era as social networking amplified desires for community but also bolstered the sense of the individual. Young people were encouraged to perform their identities online, and with the internet promising an audience, there was a sense of lonely showmanship to the whole prospect of MySpace and the blogs. It was all about you, the poster, but who was the "you" of the internet, anyway?

Kid Cudi harnessed that curious energy. He took the curves of the question of individuality and wound them up tightly. He made it cool to sulk in the increasing tension of having access to everyone, and still feeling misunderstood and trapped in your own head. "There's something to be said about the rise of the internet and social networks like MySpace," A-Trak affirms. "These new types of interactions—everyone is more connected but feels more lonely. Cudi tapped into something that was a really popular feeling around those years."

The modus operandi for Cudi in his early days saw him tapping the swelling vein of loneliness. Where *God Loves Ugly* hinged on self-deprecation, Cudi was busy unknowingly constructing a new pillar to prop up the genre. Where Atmosphere made music for the degenerate with a potential heart of gold, Cudi's music spoke to the somber everykid who was just searching for their place in the world and hoping to muster some semblance of cool as they journeyed through life. His incantations on "Day 'N' Nite" summoned the spirits of insecurity into battle with him. His persona was hewed closely to his interior, and that overlap allowed Cudi to develop emo rap into a position where emotions could still be read as pathetic, but their presentation was at least aspiring to some measure of swagger.

Kid Cudi was able to lift the hustle of "Mind Playing Tricks on Me" and the overall power of the Geto Boys to polish off the purely pathetic emo persona Atmosphere had developed. Cudi's version of the genre allowed for some playfulness. It was immediately palatable. Additionally, his visual rhetoric broke off from the dusty mire of *God Loves Ugly* and instead featured Cudi looping through a colorful, tripped-out universe. "Day 'N' Nite" would go on to telegraph the widespread appeal emo rap could have, if paired with a likable emcee and an infectious production.

"Cudi didn't originate the swaggering sad-sack archetype, but he distilled its ethos to the purest form and then rapidly saturated its influence," wrote Pranav Trewn for *Stereogum*'s ten-year retrospective on Kid Cudi's debut mixtape.[2] Trewn goes on to describe Cudi as "as much spectacle as star." With the knowledge of all Cudi has sown, there is the sense Cudi's *presence* is more valuable than the majority of his music, in much the same way Lil Wayne's presence on his rock album, *Rebirth*, is greater than the music.

"Day 'N' Nite" was not engineered to be a hit, and it's true that its edges show. Cudi's flow is imperfect. His raps sound, at times, noncommittal while his singing struggles to be more than charming. "Day 'N' Nite" sounds like a transitional space for rap. Still, it resonated with tastemakers and fans. Here was the beginning of Cudi's massive following. The writing was on the wall for emo rap when this song came out—more melody, more purplish timbre, and more plainstated writing that obscured nothing and everything at once.

When Cudi raps "the pain is deep," he is simultaneously giving himself over to the listener and saying nothing at all. The line could inspire a series of questions about trauma and how it atrophies the brain, but Cudi deadpanning the line renders those critical curiosities moot. It remains more satisfying to say, "Damn, I feel that," than it is to poke holes in the song's narrative tension. Kid Cudi establishes a literary tradition within emo rap, spotlighting this anxious dance of openness and opaque description. Where the forefathers of the genre applied a tremendous specificity to their writing, Kid Cudi's work shows the natural bends emo rap would come to adopt. As in, he creates space for the listener to become a part of the song's narrative. It is personally emergent, and it works.

"Kid Cudi made his struggle with his demons the focal point of his image," Trewn tells me. "We talk about Drake all the time, but no one points to him as defined by his emotions. Going back to Geto Boys, they have songs I'd put in my personal emo rap canon, but Kid Cudi is the first to say, 'This is my defining feature.'"

"'Day 'N' Nite' was the Godparticle of modern-day hip-hop," Trewn continues. "It was a lot of people's first exposure to this sound, and it gave rappers license—because it was very popular—to get weirder, to show more of those alternative touchpoints in their music. That song led so many artists down different paths where they wouldn't have been without it."

The slow creep of "Day 'N' Nite" was fed by a handful of successful remixes, with the Crookers's remix—which originated from a MySpace message between the Italian production then-duo and Fool's Gold—and the rap version progressively ballooning into something bigger than Fool's Gold could handle. Once Jim Jones got on a rap remix of "Day 'N' Nite," the radio potential of the song took off. "In the meantime, we had a Fool's Gold tour where Cudi was on the opening slot, performing in front of thirty people," A-Trak remembers. "Through those months, his song just got bigger and bigger."

"Somewhere along the way, Cudi's team decided to sign him to Universal/Motown," A-Trak says. "I remember, once he was signed to a major label, going to a Cudi show at South Street Seaport in New York. There was a *mob* of people screaming for him on a Beatlemania level, which is not what we were seeing just a few months ago at our homegrown event. This is a whole other story! It must've been late '08 or early '09."

As "Day 'N' Nite" grew in popularity, Cudi's touchable image endured. His humanity in those years was not washed away by the flow of capital. Instead, he doubled down on being a person-first artist. Appearances came second to the project of honesty. "People started to form a relationship with Kid Cudi," Trewn agrees. "He's sharing and documenting his journey in real time. So much of rap focuses on what you've overcome, which is so powerful. Cudi's work was set apart because he was talking about his *current* struggles. It was music for people who were fighting."

This relationship building, foundationally, makes Kid Cudi one of the icons of emo rap. His music naturally feeds into the emo sensibility of, "This music is *made for me*. I know this artist, and they know me." The truism "Kid Cudi saved my life" would go on to be mocked by critics and weaponized in online discourse, sure, but within that very sincere statement is a strain of music history: this stuff means the world to listeners.

As Cudi was able to soundtrack amorphous feelings, "Day 'N' Nite" embodied the adage, "The only way out is through." In the best way, the song and Cudi's image were shameless. There was no posturing or braggadocio that wasn't immediately met with a humbling admission of pain. The gendered subversion of "Day 'N' Nite" includes the pivot of emo rap to a more fluid form of expression. Where Slug used pain as a marker of masculinity—"I wear my scars like the rings on a pimp" is a classic Atmosphere line—Cudi embraced a more coded-feminine tone in his delivery and writing. "Day 'N' Nite" is downright gentle, from the production to the visual language.

As emo is a feminization of hardcore, Kid Cudi's landmark contribution to rap is the welcoming of such a soft bleeding out. His sensitivity opened doors for even more hysterics. Though he himself wasn't unraveling on the mic in the way artists in his wake would, Cudi was still able to establish a safe space for projecting intense emotions without having to defend masculinity. As such, Cudi allowed for the mental health conversation in hip-hop to begin taking center stage.

In 2016, Kid Cudi checked himself into rehab for depression and suicidal thoughts.[3] As reported by *The Atlantic*, once Cudi publicized his "suicidal urges," the outpouring of love on social media demonstrated the great reciprocity and humanity of emo rap, "giving rise to the hashtag #yougoodman for people to discuss race, masculinity, and depression." Here is the crux point of emo's benefit: the feeling of this music belonging to a listener allows for those listeners to rally and support their favorite artists, and each other, through difficult times and conversations.

With a demographic skewing younger, there is an awareness of artists like Kid Cudi as role models. And so his honesty in 2016 carries with it the potential to help countless listeners. The stigma surrounding mental healthcare for Black men persists in America, but as generations turn over and artists are open about their struggles as Cudi was, there is a changing tide in our perception of seeking out care.

"As I got to know and befriend the generation of rappers who came after him and saw the way they spoke about him, I could tell he was a voice for a generation," A-Trak concludes. "He made a whole bunch of teenagers feel like they were heard. I remember catching up with Cudi and telling him, 'I'm at the studio with Travis Scott.' He said he would pull up. Travis freaked out. Cudi had just bought some new sports car, and he pulled the ol', 'Get in the car, let's go for a little drive.' The three of us went and drove around, and Cudi was playing us some beats he'd just made. Travis had the excitement of a kid. When Cudi left, Travis got up on the couch and started jumping because he had just met his idol."

BONES Adds a
Gothic Texture to Emo

Elmo "BONES" O'Connor: When I went by Th@ Kid, I was not trying to be dark, I was just kicking raps about smoking or whatever. And
then I hit a point where I was like, "Okay, I'm eighteen now. I can't be
Th@ Kid any more. What's the name change? Is it going to be Th@
Guy? What's it going to be?" And I've always looked at music like
wrestling, and The Undertaker always looks like the funnest thing to
be. So, I was with my brother Justin, from Michigan, and we were like,
"We should go dark." So we decided to channel the fact that I'm a
skinny white guy with fucked-up teeth and long hair and make this
backwoods character who you'd see in an alleyway, or behind a gas
station at three in the morning—a seedy dude. So that was the core
idea, just to scare you with this boogeyman character mixed with that
'90s scumbag realism.... I fell back into old shit that we would listen
to, like The Dayton Family, Three 6 [Mafia], and old Project [Pat]. I
was like, "Dude, nobody does dark, dark now." This was around the
time A$AP [Rocky] put out [F**kin' Problems]. Everything was so
light, and then [SpaceGhost] Purrp came out with music, and Eddy
[Baker], Chris [Travis], and [Ethel (now Xavier)] Wulf. I was like, "Yes!
It's not just me that wants it to go in this direction." And that's how

we all found each other. We all liked the same shit when the scene was so small. It's cool to see how big it is now.[1]

* * *

GUTSY, GRIMY, AND CONTINUOUSLY INNOVATIVE, MICHIGAN-RAISED and Los Angeles-based rapper BONES changed the landscape of the hip-hop underground with a seedy concoction of gothic tones and an emphasis on Southern rap traditions. The artist grew up more invested in the timbre of seminal groups like Three 6 Mafia and Geto Boys than the changing landscape of rap in the 2010s. By age seventeen, while still running around as Th@ Kid, BONES released over a dozen mixtapes. Currently, the man has released over ninety albums. Under a handful of aliases, along with his joint albums and side projects, BONES has revealed himself slowly as someone capable of revising himself into iconoclast status. To his fans, he is a rap hero. To the countless artists he's influenced, he is either a north star or a distant whisper—the difference coming down to artistic pride clouding a willingness to give flowers when due.

BONES is reclusive, but no less resonant. The founder of hip-hop conglomerate TeamSESH, BONES, and members and affiliates Eddy Baker, Chris Travis, and Xavier Wulf, all played a role in defining emo rap following Atmosphere and Kid Cudi. BONES brought in an overbearing darkness that was being washed out of emo rap following the boom of Cudi's "Day 'N' Nite." Their music is heavy and entrancing, packed with rich cultural references and brooding imagery. It is verbose and deceptively dense—dizzying stuff that manages to coax the listener into a swirling, gloom-stricken underworld.

Shortly after his ninth birthday, BONES found himself downloading beats online and making "shitty raps" and R&B songs for fun. His family's music and arts history—BONES's father is a photographer, and his mother is a clothing designer who now mans the TeamSESH ware-house—inspired his tastes: early Motown records and rap classics like Master P and Lil Wayne. These influences would emerge in his work and work ethic immediately. In particular, the dent Wayne left on modern hip-hop would leak into BONES's entire oeuvre. The two artists record and release with the same fervor; they elicit a similar dedication from their fans; they make the texture of the English language, as well as its limitations and idiosyncrasies, work for them on the mic. Without Wayne, there is no blueprint for BONES, who himself would become a blueprint for an entire scene.

In his youth, there are "shitty raps" and a piqued interest. These moments serve as the prologue for BONES's career, which formally begins after a tumultuous time in high school: "Teachers wouldn't give me assignments because it would just be a waste of paper." At sixteen, BONES drops out and moves to California with his brother and manager Elliott O'Connor. Once in LA, he connects with gritty rap collective Raider Klan, meeting Eddy Baker in an internet cafe, though Eddy recalls their first meeting being a Runescape convention.[2] The move and newfound free time help BONES decide to take rap seriously. The flurry of recording and releasing in real-time begins, leading to the self-release of his first full-length project *WhiteRapper* in 2012 under the Th@ Kid moniker.

With *WhiteRapper*, Th@ Kid accomplishes something critical. Beyond charting a course for his career as BONES, beyond sparking label interest and extinguishing it in the name of forging his own path, the artist lights the fire for a new tone in emo rap. Th@ Kid debuts and adds a near-playful element to a genre that dangerously treads towards self-seriousness. In 2012, O'Connor *was* serious, but he was also *funny*. There is levity to *WhiteRapper* that was missing from Atmosphere's offerings. The jokes Slug put forward on *God Loves Ugly* kept Slug in his own crosshairs, sure, but they didn't feel completely goofy. They felt like cries for help.

When Kid Cudi broke, humor was out the window in place of a sulking and forlorn persona, and self-serious emo rap was in. So, there was something attractive about Th@ Kid's new and underdeveloped voice stepping into a familiar arena. It allowed for his charm to flower up from the imperfections of the twenty-plus songs on *WhiteRapper*. Emo rap's lexicon was expanding. *WhiteRapper* was breaking ground on a new tradition, one that would give way to some of the late Lil Peep's earliest releases: "feelz" and "Keep My Coo."

From the length to the homage on the cover—*WhiteRapper* is fashioned in the style of classic Pen & Pixel covers, best known for their design work with No Limit and Cash Money—it's clear Th@ Kid has a reverence for rap history. He just doesn't let that ferocity consume him to the point of making the music feel cumbersome. Still, this mixtape is an *effort*. It radiates a level of severity most associated with the desperation that comes with trying to make something out of nothing.

It's easy to return over a decade later and read *WhiteRapper* with a propulsive urgency, especially considering how much music would pour out of BONES in the months and years to come. Ultimately, though, *WhiteRapper* is very much a thing out of time. The unpolished tape calls on early 2000s hip-hop in form and function while still driving emo rap into the future. And while *WhiteRapper* isn't exactly the flavor of emo rap BONES would become known for, it served as a bridge for both the artist and the genre. In December 2012, BONES would shed "Th@ Kid" and make a play towards actualizing himself as an artist. He understood he was onto something bigger than he could have imagined.

By the time of BONES's entrance, there was already a divide within emo rap's aesthetic. Kid Cudi's "lonely stoner" vision for emo rap didn't align with the darkness BONES would harness. Cudi's music was angled towards giving lost kids an approachable soundtrack—"Day 'N' Nite" was bare and honest, but it was missing a sense of foreboding. It didn't bite. Cudi made emo rap draped in pastels, and BONES had no interest in stepping outside of a monochrome existence. BONES and

Atmosphere have more to do with each other than any other contemporary emo rapper and the genre's forefathers. Sure, BONES is more interested in tormented and sordid imagery than being blacked out, but he does pull from Slug's school of gross everyman presentation. BONES's works reject Cudi's gentle sensitivities, ultimately expanding listeners' conception of the genre.

WhiteRapper is laced with a thick ick. It feels slimy. That was the intent, but considering by 2012 Atmosphere's style was not the only one budding in the underground rap scene, it is an interesting starting point for BONES. Perhaps that afterimage of grime from '02 to '12 represents a truth about emo rap: it is largely nasty stuff. Raw, wounded, and outright disgusting music that jars the senses and feels like a bottomless source of negativity. BONES affirms this with the title of one of his 2013 records, *SCUMBAG*.

The brutish cousin of *sleaze*, the notion of a *scumbag* is more damning and intense. The mouthfeel of both words communicates this best: *scumbag* as a matter of language feels like hacking up stones, while *sleaze* has a drooly slickness to it. The grime, hopelessness, and muck of songs like "DeathMetal" and "GraveyardGod" are offset by the gentle tones of "Nightmare" and "DieForMe," which feature BONES hitting his upper register to accentuate the pain. The latter two tracks speak to BONES's influence perhaps even more so than the grittier cuts—he all but predicted the way singing would help emo rap move into the mainstream.

BONES released a handful of other crucial records in 2013: *CRACKER*, *PaidProgramming*, and *LivingLegend*. One of the titans of independent music blogging, *Passion of the Weiss*, published an early critical look at BONES on the eve of *PaidProgramming*'s release. "He's made the backward gaze infinitely more interesting by cloaking it in opaque fog of the undead," critic Max Bell explained. "And instead of pretending that he isn't aping '90s in 2013, it's as if he refuses to believe that he doesn't live in that decade. Above all, Bones may have created a world out of time. I don't want to live there, but it sounds like a place I'd consider visiting on Halloween."[3] This critique remains one of the most generous early writings of an emo rap artist on the rise. Where critics of early Lil Peep and Juice WRLD records struggled to make sense of the young artists' abilities, because BONES's music so directly channeled key hip-hop influences, it appeared easier to stomach and parse.

As BONES's catalog grew, so did his status as an influential artist. In 2014, BONES began getting national looks for the release of his mixtape, *Garbage*.[4] The tape hones in on BONES's aesthetic: the cover features his now-signature mucking around with VHS tape, and the music is the most concise and sharp BONES had released to that point. From a Corbin feature on "IfYouHadAZuneIHateYou" to the consistent homage to Three 6 Mafia, *Garbage* positions BONES as an artist who defies trends and will steadfastly be a "skinny white pimp named BONES, with the knife."

Garbage is clear. BONES's vocals cut through and, as a result, his violent imagery penetrates with ease. But these aren't traditional post-Eminem horrorcore raps. On *Garbage*, BONES is a skilled emotional puppeteer, stringing up complex ideas around whiteness and class alongside gruesome impulses, never allowing one feeling to collapse into another. He raps about burying someone in the mud in lurid detail, only to flip the plot and comment on his "white trash" status for levity. BONES uses the veil of calculated self-awareness to pull off a listenable balancing act. He capitalizes on sinking feelings, but never crashes.

Online and in print, he is regarded as the gothic father of emo rap. BONES is presented as a brooding and reluctant hero for a swarm of kids and aspiring artists. "Right now, Bones might be doing that better than anyone," *The FADER* wrote after the release of *Garbage*. Of course, one tape a year is not enough for BONES. As *Skinny* and *Rotten*, and others, trickled out of him in 2014, *Complex* began taking consistent notice of the rapper. For an artist with little chart appeal, this was monumental. It felt as though the blood-letting BONES was doing in the booth was paying off—his rise as the "teenage corpse" creeping through alleyways until returning to his crypt was entirely organic.

The early 2010s were a glimmering time in hip-hop. We were approaching the apex of the blog era, where fans-turned-writers used their platforms to shine lights on the music that mattered most to *them*. These outlets—*2DopeBoyz*, *DJBooth*, *NahRight*, and others—climbed out of the cracks of an industry adapting to the internet age and developed unique perspectives to help champion their favorite songs and mixtapes. Plucky, sunny, "happy rap" was in: Wiz Khalifa and Chance the Rapper released classic mixtapes in 2010 and 2013 respectively. BONES didn't care. He did not deal in the same jubilant energy as other aspiring rappers at the tail end of the blog era. By *Rotten*, BONES had solidified himself as a dark and snarling force in the underground. Some of his most recognizable songs live on the tape, including the second track, "HDMI," a booming answer to the watered-down gothic tones he heard in the likes of A$AP Rocky.

Rotten is the first essential solo BONES release. Here, the rapper explores the breadth of his range and quiets the common critique that one BONES song represents them all. The origin point of the trappy, hazy, scattershot SoundCloud rap era soon following the slow decline of the blogs can be traced to "HDMI," "Amethyst," and "Unknown" just as easily as to early A$AP Rocky mixtapes. More important to the scope of emo rap, however, is the scant dose of gentleness BONES applied to *Rotten*. "Yes,EvenThen" and "SadlyThatsJustTheWayThingsAre" are bare ballads. These two songs are some of the clearest stepping stones for the softness of Lil Peep's first mixtape, *Lil Peep; Part One*, released in the fall of 2015. *Part One* standout "five degrees" even interpolates BONES's "Cut" from 2013. With that, *Rotten* presented BONES as fearless. He wasn't just adding a few necessary wrinkles to emo rap— BONES was here as a blooming agent. A drop of his style in a pool of the genre's essence and suddenly the colors and textures have spun out into a new universe of expression.

This story continues on for ten years. With his hyper-specific aesthetic, BONES fortified his longevity. His ability to maintain a career, without tiring himself out or wearing on the ear of the listener, is a testament to the lightning he's been able to bottle hundreds of times. While there is some truth to the notion that BONES's playing in the same aural arena can lead to repetition, there is something doubly impressive about his fastidiousness. BONES is an unbothered and unshakeable force in hip-hop. And his fans love it.

The immediacy in his music—both in his recording schedule and the breathless way he attacks the mic—follows the path of Lil Wayne's 'oos mixtape era. Before the long albums and tireless drops of the streaming era became the norm, BONES was intent on unleashing twenty-to-thirty-song albums, multiple times a year, when distribution for an indie artist was still difficult. In many ways, BONES's strategy beat streaming to the punch. His work ethic is as much a part of his persona as the music, and it speaks to the fury with which emo rap can be produced and sent into the crowd.

The rate at which BONES creates allows fans into his interior life on his terms. Almost in real time, listeners witness his growth and the changes going on in the hip-hop underground without ever getting that much closer to knowing O'Connor. The promise of a subgenre and culture as intensely charged as emo rap sits neatly on relatability. When lonely nights in feel endless, and the ceiling fan is your only friend, this music becomes comfort, camaraderie. The relationship to the artist helps determine if the rap is emo—it's an ecosystem. BONES doesn't have to outwardly wail about the angst and heartbreak of being young and lost. His willingness to give and give when it comes to music is enough, inspiring a tight-knit and loyal cult following.

These diehard fans have assumed the role of archivists, running online forums and meticulously maintaining the TeamSESH discographies—keeping them accessible and organized for newcomers and veteran fans. There is an unexpected symbiosis here, how the fans perform a type of labor for BONES's legacy while BONES produces album after album to nourish fans' lives. The mutual respect between BONES and his listenership isn't unique. This type of fervor helps define emo as emo, and it is critical for the endurance of an act. The relationship exists without pretense, and BONES has frequently expressed disbelief at people enjoying his work. Instead of feeling a stark power imbalance between artist and observer, the two seem nearly on equal footing.

The fans are just as valuable to the enterprise of understanding O'Connor's material contributions to emo rap as the music. While so many crucial artists have tragically passed, their fanbases have remained steady and serious. Lil Peep and Juice WRLD tribute pages have been going strong for years, welcoming new fans and acting as safe spaces for many to mourn their losses. BONES is still alive and recording, but his fans present the same as Peep's and Juice WRLD's. Death and grief reshape minds and relationships—things feel more dire, they have more value. To that end, the response to BONES's work, the way fans interact with the material, speaks to the unending value BONES brings them. The fans work in concert with the music to establish BONES as a staple and beloved pioneer. With the rise of streaming, fans have grown ever more fickle, spoiled with choice. Still, TeamSESH feels like a lifestyle.

BONES's story is one of subversion and rebellion—here is an indie artist with no machine behind him who has a ravenous fanbase and operates at raceway speeds, setting his own rules every step of the way. He does not capitulate to the music business, ignoring pop-rap trends and staying the course of being an underground icon. Holding strong and making an aesthetic timeless is not without its pains. In the mid 2010s, BONES did a small press run where he was nothing if not capricious. He appeared hurt by the rise of artists who were all but robbing SESH of their style and teetering on achieving mainstream acclaim while, according to him, watering down the sound he helped pioneer. BONES didn't name names, but he was acerbic.

In the new decade, though, with a little more maturity and becoming a father, BONES appears far less concerned with broad notoriety—not that he ever gave the impression he was hoping to chart. There is more to BONES than music and legacy—he is a joyful family man—but even as he's discovered newfound priorities in life, the music has not suffered. He has not slowed.

In 2022, BONES released four albums, bringing together unexpected collaborations with street rappers Lil Gotit and Rio Da Yung OG for the ten-years-on sequel to cult classic tape *1MillionBlunts*, rightfully named *2MillionBlunts*. He also worked with OG TeamSESH member ghostNghoul on *DreamCard*. The music in the 2020s is just as gothic and inspired as it was in the early 2010s. BONES's output may have him forgetting his own lyrics in interviews, but it doesn't dilute the value of the material itself. Certainly, it doesn't dissolve the impact it has had on his community. BONES's catalog affirmatively answers a curious question: What would happen if we took the productive spirit of Lil Wayne, the dark tones of classic Southern hip-hop, and the seedy image of a "skinny white pimp," and thrust it into the world?

Lil Wayne's Influence on Emo Rap

BY THE MID-2010S, THE VISUAL LANGUAGE OF EMO RAP HAD BEEN defined by face tattoos, colorful hair, and a broad mix of deep purples and bright pinks. Where BONES, Atmosphere, and Kid Cudi appeared as everymen in their own lanes, this era also mandated a new-age rock star cosplay. To complement the music, artists in the canon had to adopt a style popularized by the late Lil Peep. Innovating on the look of underground hip-hop, Peep was heralded as a "fearless" fashion icon by GQ shortly after sitting front row at a Paris Fashion Week show in 2017.[1] And the imitators following his passing, the lesser and more sterile acts, borrow heavily from his handbook: copious pink, abundant strutting, and a faux-cheeky attitude.

Peep, with his boyish charm and approachable appearance as a handsome white artist, established a play-by-play of tailoring yourself in the digital underground. His vibrant sense of style set him apart from the modalities of his emo rap lineage. But it was late-2000s Lil Wayne who acts as the true molten core of the genre's visual language. "Young rappers, including young emo rappers, style themselves after him," music critic Paul Thompson explains of Wayne. "The guitar fetishization of his late-middle period plays in here. Wayne is a progenitor of a lot of this stuff."

"Prom Queen" is the obvious callout. In the song's video, Wayne is jamming on a bright red electric guitar in the vein of Lil Jon's *Crunk Rock*. He serves as an additional aesthetic origin point for Lil Peep, Lil Tracy, Trippie Redd, or any other artist interested in fashioning themselves as a bona fide emo star.

"You see Lil Wayne doing jam sessions with Fall Out Boy and Gym Class Heroes," music journalist Christina Lee recalled in an episode of the *Bottom of the Map* podcast with hip-hop scholar Dr. Regina N. Bradley.[2] "That's where you see him reach this whole other audience, and I understand. It's not that great. It's mostly the *image* of him that's so memorable. That's what people cling onto." She recalled Playboi Carti, a rage rap icon, getting a tattoo of *Rebirth*-era Wayne. "The image is almost more important than the sound."

The visuals accompanying Wayne's *Rebirth* era spawned a generation's worth of influence—red candles, red wine, scuffed Converse, colorful Vans, an ever-so displaced beanie. Wayne took the forlorn skater aesthetic Cudi developed on "Day 'N' Nite" and injected it with his New Orleans swagger. It was almost as if Wayne was handed Cobra Starship demos and couldn't shake the feeling something was *there*. Where Cudi appeared dejected, Wayne was on top of the world, having a blast garbling and warbling atop frenetic guitar riffs. Wayne's presence on *Rebirth* signaled a tonal shift for emo rap: this stuff could be *fun*. Atmosphere's records were sharp, Cudi's were bubbly but depressing, and BONES firmly spooled gothic sensibilities even at his funniest. With Wayne acting as a type of bedrock, though he wasn't exactly making emo music, there was a sense of liberation. His image represented an exercise in breaking boundaries and rewriting the rules of hip-hop adjacency.

Wayne's sudden transformation into a rock star spawned an understandable panic. It's not uncalled for—and certainly not surprising—given Lil Wayne was *the* rapper in every imaginable way in the late 2000s. In 2005, Wayne declared himself the best rapper alive. With every *Tha Carter* entry, along with the *Dedication* series, Wayne pumped out landmark moments in rap history. Late 2000s Wayne was deserving of the "meteoric" adjective, perhaps more than any rap artist before or after him.

"Lil Wayne's self-proclaimed greatness turned from bluster to truth seemingly through willpower alone," goes a 2007 *FADER* cover story by Nick Barat.[3] In 2017, Barat remarked, "It's highly unlikely Wayne will ever be the artist of the moment again," underscoring the overwhelming, inconceivable, now-untouchable significance of 2000s Wayne.[4] In 2023, Wayne, a workhorse without question, doesn't even recall the *Tha Carter* series.[5] He is too keyed into the future, fueled by his 2005 flag-planting. In an interview with *Rolling Stone*, Wayne explained, "Every single action, every single word, every single approach," is driven by maintaining his crown as the best.

And so, on the heels of Wayne's indescribable apex point in hip-hop all those years ago, "Prom Queen" was received poorly by purists. *Entertainment Weekly* took glee in bashing him.[6] "This unholy combination of bargain-basement mall-metal riffage and semi-conscious Auto-Tuned moaning sounded bad enough in the studio," the piece expounds. "'Prom Queen' would be lame if it was being played by a random rock band. It's still just as lame when it's being played by the world's biggest rapper." Wayne turning his persona into something more recognizable to mass audiences, the rejection of the Southern rap tradition in favor of something classically understood as white and suburban, is a significant touchpoint in the history of emo rap.

The critical writing surrounding the *Rebirth* era calls to mind remarks made in *VICE*, in 2016, when Lil Peep was breaking out of his SoundCloud shell: "Lil Peep is the 2016 version of mallcore: a white rapper who samples Brand New and sings about suicide."[7] Though *VICE* was kinder to Peep than *EW* was to Wayne, there is the throughline of initial confusion-turned-disgust. This was based on the material: Peep performing a goth affect was more touching, more proficient, and more part of his initial artist DNA than Wayne's playing in the same space. *Rebirth* is undoubtedly the weakest entry in Lil Wayne's discography.

"You get an alternative viewpoint that might not be a lens that is used for young Black men," Dr. Bradley said. Therein lies the supreme importance of *Rebirth*, not just to emo rap, but to all of hip-hop in the 2010s. Wayne was expanding the language and texture of hip-hop for a new generation, was broadening the creative options afforded to young Black artists, by way of his experimentation. He was not the first Black artist to adopt rock sensibilities within a non-rock genre—*Collision Course*, the 2004 collaborative mash-up album between Jay-Z and Linkin Park, exists in its own curious pantheon, and the band Gym Class Heroes is the undisputed bedrock of this Wayne Era.

Still, it is the magnitude of Wayne, his being the biggest rapper alive, the most elastic and proficient, that gives *Rebirth*'s role in hip-hop history an additional oomph. As the 2010s drew on, as more rappers adopted Wayne's *Rebirth* style and overall sonic palette, the ire they drew dampened. The response to *Rebirth* showcased just how precious Wayne's rapper image was to fans and critics, and his shattering of expectations goes down as one of the great sleights of hand in contemporary rap.

When Wayne gets bashed for "Prom Queen," there is a lot to consider between the curiosity of genre-coded expectations, the looming feeling of betrayal from rap purists, and the wonder of, "Is this stuff even good?" Does the material on *Rebirth* earn the hate, or are the arguments against the album made in bad faith? In Wayne's lineage, artists like Juice WRLD and non-emo rapper Lil Yachty adopt a desire to be seen as "artists" and not merely rappers.[8] The panic of losing tradition, of devaluing the artform of hip-hop makes sense, but also stands to limit young artists' ability to experiment. In as many ways, *Rebirth* represents a broadening of hip-hop as it does a flop for Wayne's discography. There are better emo rap offerings from Lil Wayne, stronger and more thematically rich songs that help build out the canon for the next generation of artists.

Paging through his records, it becomes clear Wayne is much more than a visual beacon for emo rap. "People will cite a given Kanye or Cudi song, but I think 'Prostitute Flange' [2007] is as stylistically influential on current emo rap as anything. Wayne got very, very comfortable being sad on records," Thompson says. "Which is strange, because he was a child star at first. You go back to 'I Miss My Dawgs,' [released in 2004] and it's the same kind of thing as emo rap. 'I am going to make a song for mass consumption, that is three letters from me to three of my former friends.' There is this sense of Wayne that gets at two chief characteristics of emo rap. The first is on a basic level, being that comfortable being that revealing on records. The second is the sense that these things are spilling out of him in real-time."

"Prostitute" in particular underscores an understanding that emo rap is a sexually driven genre—to depressing ends. The angst of wanting someone and the use of sex as a vehicle through which to prop yourself up are all key parts of capturing the roiling nature of being a teen locked away with your own thoughts. Almost every Lil Peep song involving a partner plays into the narrative arc laid out by "Prostitute." That is: "I love you so much. Please don't betray me. We should have sex, because this is how I'll express that I value you." And to the end of the final moment of this arc, sex is used to help fill in gaps of feeling these artists don't yet know how to articulate.

From Wayne's forlorn calls to keep the love real, to Peep singing the same themes nine years later on the 2016 single "Your Eyes," there's an insistence on trust being foundational. These songs are about sex, sure, but they are better understood as discussions of insecurity. There is a sense trust is easily lost, and not so easily granted. The giving and taking of pleasure in emo rap is a mask for the extreme anxiety of sharing yourself with someone. There is vulnerability in expressing the potential for a partner to hurt you, as if to say, "I know they will hurt me, I just *know* it." The expectation of betrayal is a trademark of the genre. Mindless sex, in the writing, is meant to be a shield from that betrayal, a way to suggest the artists didn't even care in the first place.

Additionally, the "real-time" aspect of Wayne's releases carries with it the same aura that followed Juice WRLD as he freestyled his way through his sophomore album, *Death Race for Love*. There is an emphasis in emo to deliver the cardinal emotion as intensely and as quickly as possible. The speed at which Peep and Juice produced music fed into their genre convention. Their work ethics reflected the promise that emo rap was a boots-on-the-ground report of despair. It also spoke to their proficiency as artists, this ability to excavate constantly and release a stream of songs ranging from listenable to addictive. Dr. Bradley and Lee discussed the prolific process of recording at length, with Dr. Bradley citing the way Wayne shattered notions of literacy for Southern Black artists by abandoning the notebook and attacking the beat off top.

"It all goes back to the standard that Wayne set," Lee added, speaking specifically to the way artists like Migos and 2 Chainz record, "which is to let the music dictate what he's gonna say, rather than coming in 'prepared.' More often than not, I've seen folks going in and doing what the beat instructs them, as set by Wayne's example. Rather than go in with a manifesto: 'this is what I'm gonna get off my chest.'"

Wayne's unmanicured approach bled into all the emo rap to follow. He opened a door for artists in the subgenre to dig deep in a manner of flow. His *Rebirth* look shaped the culture and his recording style changed the arrangement of the genre. Where Slug recounts birthing records and releasing them, Wayne goes a step further by showcasing the value of acting impulsively. This makes sense for a genre that largely feels like a series of outbursts and reactions. Wayne demonstrated the importance of having a feeling *and* responding to it in real time. Still, he appears calculated and entirely natural across most of his discography. With Wayne as their model, the most celebrated artists in this space grew to unleash an unfiltered clip of music as a stream of meticulous chaos. They would take the order and verbose texture of technically proficient hip-hop, and deconstruct it with either melody, intensity, or both pillars at once to build something new.

Xavier Wulf Brings
Memphis History to Emo Rap

Xavier "Xavier Wulf" Beard: I ain't trying to be nobody's father, but if a young man listens to my music, I'm going to tell him something that he can use to survive. I don't want to scream some stupid-ass, dumb-ass, ignorant hook in his ear the whole time about nothing.... I always knew what I could do, but I was like, 'I need to keep it like this for right now.' But—why wait? Time to pull the blade. I kept it concealed as long as I could, but I can't hold myself back anymore. But the problem is, I know what's gonna come with this. If I go back to that wild-style shit and those crazy flow patterns, I will out-rap and out-flow yo' ass. For anybody reading this interview, shaking their head and going, 'I don't know about that,' take yo' bitch ass to one of my Ethelwulf songs. And that's 2012. I was a baby doing that shit back then, so imagine now.[1]

* * *

MEMPHIS RAPPER XAVIER WULF IS ONE OF THE FOUNDING FATHERS of SoundCloud rap. Growing up on the "hard rap" of his city—most notably Three 6 Mafia—Wulf began rapping in eleventh grade after a stint of listening to oddball icon Lil B. Wulf cites 2012 as the year he figured out his sound, resulting in his earliest releases under the Ethelwulf alias, whose stringy vocal layerings and dark tones telegraphed the intensity of Xavier Wulf's music to follow. Wulf started up his home studio at the top of 2012, rapping over Konflict OD beats, and creating his first mixtape in the span of two months. Initially named after the Old English for "noble wolf," Xavier's immediate confidence in himself was palpable.

A former member of rap collective Raider Klan, Wulf brought classic 1990s Memphis phonk to the 2010s rap landscape. He was introduced to the Klan by Key Nyata and later invited to join by founding member SpaceGhostPurrp. "Basically, we all love the phonk man," Wulf shared in 2012.[2] "Straight like that. Like the old school nineties stuff, like dudes you probably don't even know from the nineties that we all listen to, people these days don't listen to all that. We hate the way 2012 fools rap, like we hate the way these dudes rap these days. We're cool with a few artists. Like I like Danny Brown, Odd Future—Earl all them—and you know just a few more people after that. We don't really like this era of music, so we're just doing our thing [to] bring the phonk back. That's the one thing about the Klan, we're all bringing the phonk."

Phonk itself has a subset of subgenres, but the defining characteristics lie in the cutting drum patterns and brooding basslines. Beyond Memphis rap history, Wulf declares a spectrum of influences, including "Mystikal, Korn, Gangsta Pat, Bizzy Bone, Juicy J, Koopsta Knicca, Japanese anime music, Enya, Friendzone."[3] A skater kid, Wulf was turned onto rock music by a fellow skater in the seventh grade. The music stuck to his ribs, the folds of his brain, and, in tandem with phonk, has shaped the core of his sound. The sprawl of visual and sonic signatures making an impression on Xavier facilitated the early development of his flow—in his first in-person interview, he likened this to the creation of a raw energy.[4] "You can't fight the beat," he said. "I don't rap—I decorate music."

Early single "Dark Destruction" borrows heavily from Wulf's Memphis roots: gruesome imagery, pained delivery, and dark visuals. "I'm working for my life, but I know I'm not alright," he raps. As Ethelwulf, Xavier deals with the angst of daily struggle. There is a heft to the song, undercut only slightly by Wulf's uneven flow. The song is unintentionally charming. Still, there is a strong sincerity: he sounds serious and dedicated to rap. With his staccatoed flow, there's an obvious reverence to his city's hip-hop history. On the YouTube page for the video, Xavier left a telling comment: "Ethelwulf did not curse once. yet still so dark." Humor aside, Wulf's comment speaks to the balance good emo rap must strike between gloomy scenes and raw writing. As Wulf would go on to say in an interview with *Our Generation Music*,[5] "when the listener hears [the music], they *feel* it.... You have to—this is the most important—it has to *sound* good."

On March 6, 2012, Ethelwulf released his debut mixtape, *The Wolf Gang's Rodolphe*. Each song unspools a portion of Wulf's personal hell. The playground of Southern production signatures and Wulf's tinny register drives the music—as well as his overwhelming conviction. *Rodolphe* bursts with wanton passion. As with all great debuts, there's an urgency; as if Wulf is at a life-or-death crossroads. The backing melodies on "Blunts on My Mind" are an eerie fall wind. His swagger on "Black Magic" pulses against a shapeshifting beat. "Watch Yoo Back" waterfalls syrupy notes into even more breathless raps.

"We don't care about being lyrical, that's not what's important," Wulf said. "You know how it is when that beat gets into your body, and you feel that shit in your bones? That's the thing about old school music, they didn't care about being lyrical.... It's funky, it's lo-fi. We don't give a fuck about crisp clean sounds, we don't give a damn about the mainstream. We're anti-mainstream, fuck the mainstream, we don't need a fuckin' hardass engineer. I engineer all my own music, first of all. I record my shit, I mix my shit, and I put my shit out. I don't need nobody touching my shit straight up."

The rejection of polish falls in line with sentiments from the hard-core and emo scenes of the early 2000s, where "selling out" was a sin. In addition to being a direct link to the Southern rap tradition that is the backbone of emo rap's soundscapes, Wulf is also pulling from a rock lineage in how he maneuvers as a creative. He and BONES each embody the essence of what it means to be punk, and their resilience and success in the music industry is—beyond just being shocking given the flow of the streaming era—proof positive of an appetite rap fans have for unabashed independence.

Almost exactly a year later, operating as Ethelwulf, Xavier released *Damare Shizukani*, a five-track tape emphasizing Wulf's resistance to trends and just being "cool by my damn self," as he says on opener "Tamashi." The tape's Japanese title translates to "shut up, be quiet," and precedes the *Shut Up And Listen* EP by eight months. By the release of *Shut Up And Listen*, Wulf had grown into his rap name. "I've always liked my real name since I was a kid," Wulf said in 2014.[6] "I got serious to a point within my music—I wanted to be taken serious, and I'm serious about my music and the way I sound and shit. I wanted to be known for *me*."

A dense haze blankets *Damare*, like thick fog in a haunted forest. On "Kurokumo," Wulf elevates the spirituality laden in his gothic flavor of emo rap, underscored by the holy howls. It's the most poised he's sounded on the mic to-date. These early Ethelwulf standouts are bridges between the blunt raps of Atmosphere that put emo rap on the map and the genre's cloudy future. The piano-driven production choices coil up alongside chaotic electronic accents, as on "Dengen," and make for an out-of-body experience. *Damare*'s drums have a familiar trappy feel, but the twinkling sounds in the periphery leave you feeling like you've been hurled into an intense body high.

"When I made Ethelwulf shit, that was some crazy shit," Wulf reflected in 2017.[7] "My Ethelwulf shit was really Three 6-influenced, but still metal. Still punk. Then, I got older and made the transition from Ethel to Xavier, and that's me growin' up. Still crazy, but more of a collected crazy."

In emo rap, the compulsion to break the barrier between performer and self correlates directly to the way the genre feels uniquely personal to each listener. Emo artists necessarily *belong* to their fans, and when Xavier Wulf donned his current artist name in a bid to be his most authentic self, he entered into a crucial lineage that spans the history of music. That is, he gave himself over to the listener. The value of naming in rap is crucial, and as rap names have changed over time to be less fantastical, so too have the relationships between fans and artists. Even outside of emo rap, with the flow of social media marketing pushing artists to give more and more of themselves to fans, there is a wave of unmasking happening in hip-hop. As the digital landscape of the music industry evolves, the genre of overcoming and triumph is being asked to simultaneously stop putting on airs and deal in exaggerations fit for the most gluttonous of voyeurs. The wild antics and subsequent legal fallout of rapper 6ix9ine are a prime example of this manifesting in an extreme case.

Authenticity itself is a performance, and draws up the question of who, exactly, is the arbiter of what is and isn't real. Emo rap has the propensity to be taken as literally as possible, in part because emo writing is so navel-gazing, and as well because it's dominated by young, white artists who draw from coded-white rock songs. Wulf's place in the genre is unique. He has a longstanding love for punk, fusing it with his East Memphis roots.

"I get the most emotional feeling from that—guitars, drums, all that goes crazy," Wulf said in a 2018 interview with *Pigeons & Planes*. By that time, Wulf had over half a decade in hip-hop under his belt, had moved on from the rowdy Florida collective Raider Klan, and had linked up with emo rap pioneer BONES and formed the superteam of Seshollowaterboyz. Alongside BONES, Chris Travis, and Eddy Baker, Wulf rose to underground prominence with his melancholy and honest music. No image too dark, no emotional subject too taboo, "I'd say punk rap is me, because when I do shows and aggressive music, I think about those bands that made me feel that type of way when I was a kid," Wulf said.

The music that blew Wulf's mind in middle and high school, like Korn, Slipknot, and blink-182, took on a bigger role in his work, making 2013's *Lame* a primordial soup of emo rap. "Ki Capsules" features the staggered flow Wulf was becoming known for, matched perfectly to the deep bass drums driving the song. Other fine details on *Lame*—the opening chords of "Bloody Gown," the ghostly voices on "After Death," the rushing delivery Wulf employs on "Blood Rain"—help build up to Xavier Wulf's first apex: *Blood Shore Season 1*. The one-two punch of "East Memphis Maniac" into "Public Announcement" is dizzying. The former song carries the clarity and confidence that marks a growing emcee, while "Public Announcement" borrows from the "Dark Destruction" and Ethelwulf playbook with a newfound brute force cadence.

As Xavier Wulf developed his flavor of punk rap, he injected more and more of himself into his music, particularly leaning into anime influences and love of cars, building himself up in his music as an anime character. Consequently, Wulf's music became more heartfelt and resonant. "The beat is the world," he told *Mass Appeal*.

The blaring guitars that open 2015's *Project X* capture the sheer adrenaline rush of Xavier's music. You're immediately thrown into Wulf's obsessions. You can feel the electricity of taking a tight corner, leaving skid marks, and dusting everyone around you. Wulf treks through a rolodex of anime influences with his booming voice. The samples across the tape, all pulled from anime *Initial D*, help build a cohesive world. On "Akina Speed Star," the closing sample goes, "A better engine isn't automatically gonna make the car a better machine." Given the pride Wulf has over his independence and path in the industry, this sample choice feels like a subtle flex. No amount of gear and money can substitute for talent.

On "1st Summer Night," Wulf continues a cursory exploration into the impact singing could have on his music. The song hews closely to the more immediately familiar emo rap of the 2010s while still retaining that chopping and gnawing flow that makes Xavier's music distinct. The reward of *Project X* comes from those smooth transitions and the thoughtful use of *Initial D*'s score. It is an uncompromising body of work—a reminder that Wulf, Hollow Squad, and this vein of emo rap are not interested in trends.

Wulf has evolved into a legend to his legion of fans. The meticulously maintained online communities dedicated to him and his Seshollowaterboyz comrades is a testament to what Wulf means to listeners. The Wulf archives are thoughtfully maintained, ranging from rare records, to live material, to merch, to the general sharing of moving stories among the community. To call it a cult following feels like an undersell of just how active and hands-on the fans are and how reciprocal the relationship appears to be. Wulf has a pure view of his fans—and of his impact on listeners. "If you look at my supporters, a lot of these kids are artists," Wulf told *Pigeons*. "They're amazing, smart kids. I pull a different type of situation out of people.... I'm telling you, it's a different type of situation. I've got a responsibility out here with this shit."

Concert footage from a Raider Klan tour in 2013 shows the early command Wulf had on his fans.[8] Performing at Slim's in San Francisco with a mob of people behind him on stage, Wulf summons an outsized energy from the crowd. A sea of rap hands and bodies barreling into each other speaks to the immediate connection Wulf developed with fans. There was a need for this music, this flavor of emo rap that brings the pulse of the 1990s back into view for a new generation.

Wulf remains a key inspiration for artists in his wake—including Lil Peep, who scored a Xavier Wulf feature on his 2016 mixtape *HELLBOY*. Without question, Wulf is a pillar of emo rap's existence in the 2010s. His Memphis roots help tie the genre together, and though aesthetically there's a gulf between Juice WRLD's heartbroken wails and Wulf's guttural howls, one would not exist without the other.

"It was probably Xavier Wulf," multi-Platinum Internet Money founder Taz Taylor says of his early memories of emo rap. "I remember people getting hip to him through SoundCloud. That's where it started for a lot of people." As a frequent and close collaborator of Juice WRLD, these connections between musicians cannot be understated. Juice would go on to be one of the biggest artists in the mainstream canon, but he is not a foil to Wulf. They work together to validate the genre. "There's a reason we the underground legends," Xavier Wulf told MONTREALITY during a spirited interview with the rest of Seshollowaterboyz.[9]

"For the most part, [the underground rap scene] is doing alright," Wulf said in 2017. "It has progressed, because labels have started to figure out what the fuck is going on.... Now, they're trying to catch onto it and see how they can finesse.... I'm OG in that shit—you don't go into the underground without knowing Wulf. That's a beautiful thing."

Pointing to Wulf, and then reaching further back to Memphis rap history, gives emo rap stronger legs within hip-hop's fifty-year existence. This is in direct contrast to the -coreification of new music genres in the 2020s, and how communities are being formed and named before they can establish a history.

"The internet changes microscenes really fast," *Pitchfork* writer and editor Cat Zhang tells me. "It also makes it a lot—the process of branding a scene is now really quick. If your scenes are more based in real life, it takes a while for it to be a thing, and to give it a name. It doesn't take that long for something to get a '-core' slapped on, even if it doesn't have a coherent identity. That gets branded as a microscene, but there might not even be a real scene. Then it disappears into the ether."

Xavier Wulf's prolific output and grounded lineage fights against the fizzing feeling of -cores Zhang describes. There is meat on the bones of emo rap thanks to Wulf's unwavering dedication to Memphis—and to his craft. "You can't do Memphis music unless you a Memphis dude," he told *Pigeons & Planes*. "The attitude and shit, it's just genuinely authentic. I make the type of music I make and it's not really hard. I just do me. I do Memphis."

Yung Lean Expanded
the Definition of Emo Rap

WHEN SWEDISH RAPPER YUNG LEAN'S 2013 BREAKOUT HIT "GINSENG Strip 2002" dropped, most everyone wondered if he was kidding. From the video of a baby-faced Lean moving like a poorly programmed cyborg to the absurdist writing, the song played like a digitally devised cosmic horror. There was no telling then how influential the song would become, charting a new course for emo rap and launching the tragedy-laced career of a misunderstood genre pioneer.

"Ginseng Strip 2002" splits the difference between disconcerting and being a terminally interesting curio. It's not exactly an emo rap song, skewing closely to Lil Peep's 2015 "feelz," another uncomfortably funny canonical entry for a genre pioneer—but it has many of emo's stylistic signifiers, such as dallying, drug-infused vocal performances spliced between affirming attempts at straight rapping. It would become the modus operandi for Yung Lean's entire persona in the early years, melding together morbid curiosity and utter disdain.

Lean began making mixtapes at age eleven in Sweden: "most of the songs sounded like we were trying to be Eminem."[1] His early released material was pastel-infused and psychedelic, with some forthcoming playfulness that turned into a series of partially panicked articles about what a white rapper from Sweden might mean for the future of hip-hop's purity.[2] On "Ginseng Strip 2002," Lean splits into two halves, one obsessed with his sexual acumen, the other focused on the shining future of his singing.

For the raps themselves, like many of emo rap's enduring heroes, Lean reaches into the pit of Lil Wayne's style, coupled with purplish aesthetics. The added twist being Yung Lean, the Swedish Sad Boy also influenced by depressing 50 Cent songs and (again) Geto Boys' "Mind Playing Tricks on Me." This lineage makes sense. It should have been a signifier Lean was a serious enough artist finding his way. But his early results were weak, to the point of being curiously unnerving at best and "creating unwitting caricatures of [his role models] and not much more," at worst.[3] It would take Lean a few years of constant recording, obsessive tweaking, and some abject tragedy to really come into his own as an emo rap icon—whether or not he intended to become one.

"I just work with my gut feeling," Yung Lean told *Pigeons & Planes* in 2016. "I like keeping themes for songs and try not to get sidetracked by my influences. If I listen to too much Future or 21 Savage, I can hear them in my head when I'm rapping, so I try to get them away and I just find my own voice. I dunno, I guess my approach is Daniel Johnston mixed with a Lil Wayne."

Lean—living and coping with bipolar disorder as Daniel Johnston did—saw himself in the work of the Houston indie musician. His biggest song may have been music in an Apple commercial, but Johnston was a prototypical bedroom act. Listening to his 1983 record, *Hi, How Are You*, there are parallels between the emotional chaos of that "unfinished album" and Lean's disorganized early writing. There is delightful and uneasy surprise to *Hi, How Are You*, which relates back to Lean's delivery on "Ginseng Strip 2002" and, later, "Kyoto." It is relatively common for emo rap artists to pull from this flavor of influences, be it the late Juice WRLD's infatuation with Warped Tour bands and classic rock, or Peep's sprawling affection for punk. Still, to have Lean so immersed in obscure American touch points feels pure in spite of the results of his early releases. There is the sense Lean came to this music honestly and with a sense of wonder.

Yung Lean did not conjure his sound alone. His Sad Boys crew is equally responsible for expanding the potential of emo rap's aural presence. In a 2014 interview with "Ginseng Strip 2002" producer and friend Gud, the Stockholm-based beatmaker rattles off touchpoints from death metal to psychedelic trance, which the young artist eventually began making himself in his early tweens.[4] Similarly, in 2014, Sad Boys producer Yung Sherman revealed the almost comically simplistic origins of the crews' name, citing placing "really sad" in his Sound-Cloud song titles as the catalyst.[5]

Later, in 2016, Drew Millard wrote of Gud's relationship to Lean's growth as a rapper for *Noisey*: "Gud's beats played a big role in Lean's hard-to-pin-down appeal, his lush, melodic instrumentals serving up a beguiling counterpoint to the rapper's limited range."[6] Still, those early interviews with the Sad Boys had an air of rebellion to them—one moment with *The FADER* resulted in Sherman and Gud saying repeatedly that they were bored of Sweden. There was a restlessness to the boys that revealed itself in their music.

During Gud's first-ever interview, he was posed a valuable question as to why a band of white kids from Sweden were invested so heavily in a uniquely Black artform, especially considering their flavor of rap clearly pulls from Southern hip-hop. Gud's reply ("I have to admit that, at least for me, it started with A$AP Rocky") speaks to the power of the internet in shaping taste and trends in the early 2010s, especially when "bored" teenagers are looking for an escape from their personal malaise. In the 2020 Yung Lean documentary, *In My Head*, Lean shares that he viewed the Yung Lean project as a place into which he could escape.

Returning to influences, Rocky, a Harlem rapper who was undeniably a student of DJ Screw and classic Houston soundscapes, helped bring those hazy Southern sensibilities to the forefront of the blog era—allowing them to become more and more globalized—and the New York mixtape scene. He, alongside Lil B and Clams Casino (who worked with Rocky on the classic *LIVE.LOVE.A$AP* mixtape), pioneered a sound commonly referred to as "cloud rap." In 2021, Clams reflected on his work with Rocky: "I guess that ended up inspiring kids, who knew they could make something that moved the people without the need for a bunch of expensive studio equipment. It wasn't about the quality anymore, but the feeling."[7] This feeling is what Lean siphoned and made distinctly emo rap.

Where A$AP Rocky was focused on swagger, using his music to elevate himself as the coolest person in the room, Lean's work had an emphasis on being near-pathetic. Between his mixtape *Unknown Death 2002* (2013) and his debut album *Unknown Memory* (2014), Lean meekly attempts to establish himself as something other than humorous. His odd jokes and discordant writing redefine what self-deprecation looks like for emo rap in the internet age.

Slug of Atmosphere spent 2002 lacerating himself on *God Loves Ugly* before critics could highlight his shortcomings. Lean presented a new challenge. His early works gave the floor to critics, giving them license to do the flogging for Lean who was still really sad on the tracks but in a more holistic way. Where early emo rap was less about a general mood and more focused on the writing, Lean created an emo atmosphere.

Unknown Memory was panned upon release. Still, there was *something* to the presence of the work. Lean and Sad Boys' shameless-borrowing-bordering-on-copying of the cloud-rap style and blending it with accidental kitsch made for music that was just peculiar enough to warrant repeat listens. There is a moment in the video for lead single "Yoshi City," produced by Gud, where Lean is walking alone through a dark mine shaft. It's theatrical for sure, but there's a chilliness to the scene. It feels as if Lean is about to brave the unknown world with no one by his side—though it only lasts a few moments before he is joined by his crew in a more traditional rap video setting. Even then, sitting on top of an expensive car with his friends, as Lean mimes the words, you can see him struggling to not burst out laughing.

The hook on "Yoshi City" is telling: "I'm a lonely clown, with my windows down." The writing is emo as we've come to understand it in hip-hop by the 2010s, but also funny and deeply self-aware as Lean calls himself a clown over and over with his jokey affect. This imagery recalls Atmosphere's long-running *Sad Clown* series, which dates back to 2000. There are attempts to come off as fly as A$AP Rocky's persona, cruising with the windows down, but it's near impossible to buy into Lean as anything other than kidding. His emotions are sincere, but his messy delivery recalls "Ginseng Strip" and the judgmental curiosity of, "Is this guy for real?" Lean's execution is scattered, but the single is hard to shake. And that is to say nothing of Gud's beat, which inspires pops of reddish color while managing to be cold and lonesome. The Sad Boys' secret weapon was worldbuilding.

Lean's entry into hip-hop's consciousness was met with a fresh ire, but that did not deter him. Despite the critical hatred, success came quickly, and Yung Lean would soon find himself on the precipice of a complete, nearly irreversible breakdown. A 2016 feature with *The FADER* begins, "Yung Lean was in a mental hospital around this time last year."[8] In 2015, just two years after "Ginseng Strip 2002," Jonatan Leandoer Håstad found himself in Miami, working on his third full-length album, *Warlord*, and heavily using a smattering of drugs from Xanax to cocaine to make daily life more manageable—but the highs eventually turned to intense bouts of paranoia and bloody, physical outbursts.

In My Head also focuses greatly on the wounds and aftermath of Miami, from Lean having a gruesome psychotic break to the tragic death of his US manager and friend Barron Machat in April of 2015. Following Lean's hospitalization in 2015, he returned to the Swedish countryside for a few months, recovering with his family beside him. A bipolar diagnosis came after several manic episodes. Finally, according to his mother, the diagnosis provided a sense of relief—this could be treated, managed; there were *options*. And while *In My Head* is as close to the artist as any piece of media on Yung Lean out there, the greatest moment of the documentary comes when his mother, shown after a family meal Lean prepared, says that Yung Lean chose life—and came to understand that drugs were not what made him creative. The creativity came from within. In addition to adding a wrinkle to the texture of 2010s emo rap, Yung Lean also became a stand-in for what it might mean to overcome the darkest of demons. Few artists in the emo rap canon can be looked upon in this way, and Lean's endurance and creativity is a credit to his fastidious commitment to his health.

As I write this, I am overwhelmed by gratitude to be able to remark on Yung Lean in the present tense. Lean has been on record saying he is grateful and lucky to be alive following the first two years of his fame, the rampant drug use, psychosis, and untreated bipolar disorder. All signs pointed towards Lean's untimely end. To be able to regard him as a key player in the genre, as someone who survived the cruelty of the music industry and how it wrings out the sanity and health of its brightest stars, is incredible. During the closing narrative arc of *In My Head*, there is a scene in the countryside in which Lean, Sherman, and Gud are sitting outside and discussing the "rock star" life of their early days. Sherman appears reticent when asked if he recalls the damning past, but Lean appears lucid—he welcomes the lessons learned and is evidently proud to have not become a lesson himself.

Being a literal outsider to American rap traditions, Lean ultimately provided a fresh perspective with 2016's *Warlord*, a deeply personal and overtly aggressive offering. The finished record (a demo version of the album was released, much to Lean's displeasure, by his late US manager's father) is intense and positions Yung Lean as a serious artist. These thirteen searing songs are underpinned by unfettered agony. They telegraph the future of emo rap as something potentially embroiled in electronic cacophony, borrowing heavily from that groundwork of Clams Casino and Lil B.

Lean's soundstage felt brand new. Plotting Yung Lean on a genre timeline immediately became challenging as *Warlord* complicated the definition of Lean's sound. From here, every Lean song felt like a daring question.

Lean's production choices were—and remain—unique to his oeuvre, but his delivery was familiar as the years went on. *Warlord* was released just a few months after Lil Peep's first defining work, *LIVE FOREVER*. While Peep's ear skewed more goth, both young men had a similar untrained vocal style and penchant for addled, suicidal, and, at times, loosely confident speakers on their songs. It seemed the artists represented two sonic paths to follow: one glitchy and tonally abrasive, and the other more looming and dark.

Warlord was dark in its own right, between the harsh mental state Lean was in during recording, and his eventual his hospitalization. The crowning achievement on the album, the harrowing "Miami Ultras," "was composed not in the studio but on the pier beyond it" during a full moon. On the cut, Lean sounds possessed by his very real demons. It feels as though the fabric of Lean's psyche is being finely grated into dust. There's a real sense of torment to "Miami Ultras" that was otherwise missing from emo rap in 2016—a close analog is the gothic spirit BONES embodies, but even so, his works didn't feel as dire as the work Lean was putting into the world.

Within the differences between Yung Lean and Sad Boys, and other stalwarts like BONES and his TeamSESH collective, is an expanded definition of the genre. That is, Lean helped a new branch of emo rap erupt; he gave the genre a new body. Lean proved you could be a tortured emo practitioner and also be inventive and irreverent. He and his Sad Boys crew helped to establish a sect of emo that strayed from the pop-punkish and mall-goth energy dressing up the genre in the early and mid-2010s a la Lil Peep. Lean took the foundational grossness of

Atmosphere records and turned it into a crumbly personal reckoning. In comparison to *Unknown Memory*, *Warlord* comes across as humorless and heavy. In comparison to "Ginseng Strip 2002," "Miami Ultras" feels like a portal into a new world.

However, it is important to underscore that Lean's best work came following his treatment. It would be all too easy to read into the arc of Yung Lean's mental health and drug use and determine that good art can only come from abject suffering. Instead, as Lean proved by beginning the jonatan leandoer96 project, reflection is far more powerful for art than reaction.

Psychopath Ballads is a twenty-minute course of suffering and reflection on excess, as on "Never Again." The straight rock song "Primal Fear" plays like a song out of time, like a Rites of Spring demo. Even the deceptively easy "Rockstar," where he sings of being "caught up in the wind," plays like a scrawling journal entry in which leandoer is trying to make sense of the mess of his present life. This side project under his given name expanded Lean's ability to be creative and tender without having to touch the emotionally charged scope of the Yung Lean enterprise following the trauma of 2015. Giving himself creative outlets, allowing him to draw clear lines between Jonatan the person and Lean the character, demonstrated his recovery.

By 2017's *Stranger*, released as Yung Lean, he had ascended as a songwriter. Lean was able to step away from the imaginative fantasy of his earlier works, take the darkness of his experiences, and create truly affecting music. It was less of a curiosity, but still unprecedented for emo rap. The two key songs on *Stranger*, "Red Bottom Sky," perhaps his best vocal performance, and the killer "Agony," are both poignant ballads. "Agony" stands as Lean's most affecting song to date, an incredibly self-aware tune that tugs at the threads of psychiatric despair and reflects upon them with wisdom. The simple hook, "Isolation caved in," paired with painfully honest writing about hallucinations makes this a soul-baring apex in Lean's career. "It's about being alone in a big marble house with white marble floors filled with burning golden candles and everything comes alive when you're alone," Lean shared with NPR.[9]

These songs still draw tears from crowds and Lean himself as he performs on festival stages. Even if Lean doesn't regard himself as a leader in the emo rap scene, watching performance footage, seeing fans fly in from across the world to his show to ultimately cry their eyes out in the front row, speaks to the uniquely emo sensation of an artist belonging to their fans. Much like Lil Peep's early concert footage accentuated the dissolution of performer and audience, Lean—at every level of his fame and career—appears to be one with his fans. At the least, that's how the fans see things.

"I was definitely ahead of my time, but I don't think I single-handedly changed the route of modern hip-hop," Lean remarked in 2020.[10] When asked about the larger emo rap scene, Yung Lean seems uncomfortable making sweeping statements. Perhaps this is humility or a desire to be as historically accurate as possible, or a mix of both. Lean's uneasiness in celebrating his and his friends' legacy is also indicative of how quickly music history moves in the internet age. Collectives, genres, subcultures, and -cores form and disband rapidly. People rush to cover scenes' histories before the members of those movements even have a chance to identify themselves, what they've done, or what they're hoping to accomplish. The anxiety of being first overtakes the importance of giving cultural oddities room to breathe.

Still, Lean's impact is felt, and perhaps most visible in an emo rap artist like 6 Dogs, who came up through SoundCloud. The late 6 Dogs was a fervent fan of Yung Lean's entire discography, with the earlier works and MGMT deep cuts influencing his final album, *RONALD.*, completed before 6 Dogs's passing but released posthumously. 6 Dogs's eponymous debut tape has Lean's fingerprints all over it. Lean's impact is felt between 6 Dogs's ear for curious production and the slight deadpan in his delivery, which is upended mid-song by melodic accents time and time again on the tape. "Faygo Dreams" is a gentler version of "Ginseng Strip 2002." There is a softness to "Faygo Dreams," a sense of overcoming: "I'm thankful for these scars." While 6 Dogs was an artist with a clear and expansive vision, his roots in Lean's school of emo rap tether him to a larger tradition.

"I realized, influence, it's like a tree," Lean said in October 2022.[11] "It has all these roots. So a Soulja Boy song might be influenced from OJ da Juiceman and Gucci Mane, but when it comes out, it's Soulja Boy's way of thinking. Nothing really is made in a vacuum. You can look at black metal, and you know it comes from Black Sabbath and Iron Maiden. It's just a Nordic version of it. I love music when you know that someone's trying to do something, but it comes out the other way. Dizzee Rascal, he said it in an interview, he's like, 'I just wanted to sound like Three 6 Mafia.' And Dizzee Rascal sounds completely different. I think it's interesting to be open, and be like, yo, for what I'm doing right now, I'm listening to a lot of Prince. Obviously, it's not going to sound like Prince, but still, it's good to say what you're inspired by. I think the best musicians always listen to a lot of music."

Within this quote is perhaps the most interesting fact of Yung Lean's presence in emo rap: he was a minor Houdini. His latest works in the early 2020s and late 2010s are much more interested in pop experimentation than they are in advancing emo rap into a new decade. Lean appeared suddenly, expanded the definition of emo rap with his friends, and, just as quickly, escaped into something new. It wasn't exactly a pilfering of the genre; rather, Lean's magic act spoke to the flow of influence in the digital age, how you can mean so much to a movement without intending to.

Lean's got roots in emo rap—he planted them himself. But what has grown out of his early work is a series of wonderfully sideways projects, culminating in 2022's *Stardust*, which is his most daring mixtape to date. On it, Lean heats, stretches, bends, and breaks apart conceptions of his prior work, while maintaining his distinct vocal signatures. The tape sees the once "lonely clown" establish himself beyond the otherwise nebulous idea of *something more*, rolling the putty of his early potential between his fingers, and ultimately throwing it out the window as he instead sculpts with fire.

Chasing the Light
of 6 Dogs's Legacy

Chase "6 Dogs" Amick: I just needed an outlet. I've always wanted to rap.... Literally if I didn't start recording I [would] have killed myself by now, not even kidding. It's insane what a difference it made. It's just getting everything out there. I had a therapist at one point and that's nice, being able to tell things to someone, but when you tell things to literally everyone on the internet it's amazing. It's like having a million therapists.[1]

* * *

THE FIRST 6 DOGS INTERVIEW COMES OUT IN EARLY MARCH 2017, following the viral success of his second-ever recorded song, "Flossing." In the video, 6 Dogs is out of focus and underexposed, holding cough syrup, and dancing meekly in front of a projection of the *One Piece* anime title card and, eventually, Kurt Cobain. The visual is a compendium of being extremely online and unhappy. The sung-spoken "Tell my mom that I'm sorry" anchors the song's glimmering sorrow.

6 Dogs managed to take the stark misery of emo rap and layer it atop a softly sunny production. "Flossing" spoke to the tangle of emotions

and sputtering quality of being a teen in the 2010s. Of course it went viral. At seventeen, 6 Dogs recorded his first interview, without his mom knowing, while indefinitely grounded. This gentle punk energy was the ethos of the young artist from his first tracks recorded in an Atlanta suburb at his neighbor's house, to his final album *RONALD.*, completed before his untimely passing in January 2021.

Amick landed on his artist name after dog motifs showed up across a series of freestyles with his cousin when he was ten years old. That, or he was pulling from a traumatic experience from an even earlier time, when he was chased by a group of dogs while riding his bike. Unsure of the origin point himself, what Amick was certain of, however, was his future. "I always wanted to be a rapper," Amick said in a 2018 interview with No Jumper.[2] "I never had the confidence, and then, at a certain point, you just gotta be like, *who fucking cares*? Got the confidence. I was sitting down, eight hours a day, thinking about being a rapper."

6 Dogs grew up in a religious household, learning Bible verses and being homeschooled before entering a private Christian school from third to fifth grade. In subsequent interviews, Amick spoke to how these teachings prompted him to be more interested in "oneness," rather than organized religion. His parents' views of his career were mixed to start, but by 2018 they were thrilled with his success.

"'Flossing,' I was into Oxycontin and stuff.... I got arrested in high school, and my mom found out about my music at the exact same time," 6 Dogs said during a HAM Radio interview.[3] "It was a huge, perfect storm that just blew up in my face."

The arrest and probation were conduits for Amick, allowing him to "chill out" and reset his substance use and behavior. Consistent personal growth and learning became pillars of his personality. As the HAM Radio interview turned to his mushroom use, Amick spoke to the importance of being intentional as you approach psychedelics and life in general. Lucidity radiated off of him. Like most emo rap, 6 Dogs's music was quickly written off as goofy, but there was a surprising depth to the entire package.

6 Dogs's music was as playful as it was depressive, as rowdy as it was melodic. His songs were starfields of the tension between being young, hurt, and intent on getting through it all. His voice was light on the ear, and though those early tracks—"Flossing," "Demons In The A," "Faygo Dreams"—had the wobbly presence of a new artist, there was an undeniable charm to his delivery. Still, Amick had gone on record several times saying he ultimately came to dislike "Demons In The A" because it was little more than a moment of posturing over a trap beat. He was still finding his footing on "Flossing." But, listening closely, there was something seismic. 6 Dogs's music flourished with the same natural charisma as Lil Peep and Yung Lean, two major influences, allowing digital crate diggers to look past the technical flaws and place bets on Amick as the "future" of a burgeoning sound.

Released in the summer of 2017, the self-titled *6 Dogs* mixtape would go on to become a touchstone of the digital underground. The tape was at once a signal of shifting tides in the new Atlanta rap scene, and a personalized 6 Dogs philosophy textbook. Amick was pulling from his childhood and early adolescent experiences to make something universal. He dealt in looping imagery and pained specificity, all to the end of making thought-provoking and honest music. "I like to think of God as a common man" opens the mixtape, setting up the listener to pursue spirituality. As with the late Lil Peep, whose writing revealed itself to be hyperspecific the closer listeners grew to Gus himself, 6 Dogs's first major release had a deeply personal touch that unraveled as fans dug into Amick's crystalizing worldviews. *6 Dogs* saw the rapper hurl heavy thoughts, leaving mighty craters for the listener to tour and excavate.

6 Dogs's self-titled tape brings to mind the photographer Robert Frank's *The Americans*, which was initially bashed by critics because the images obscured critical focus and felt, much like Atmosphere records, gross. *6 Dogs* was less gross than Atmosphere; it was more in tune with

Yung Lean's brand of emo rap, with the perceived sloppiness of *The Americans*. Both works were easy to pick on, easy to relegate as a collection of errors.

Yet, in its ability to transcend technicality, letting grit and grain do the talking, *6 Dogs* would become a beacon for a new generation of underground, digitally minded rappers. 6 Dogs ensured the pursuit of perfection would never overshadow the art. Every song on *6 Dogs* does the important work of elevating who Chase was, and to where he could astrally project himself. Even at his lowest, as on "Flossing," made in response to the grueling high of mixing Oxycontin and cough syrup, 6 Dogs' music was future-minded.

"I ended up getting out of that mindset, and that's where 'Faygo Dreams' comes from: 'I'm thankful for these scars,'" 6 Dogs said in his No Jumper interview. He quickly understood his music could not only exist in an ecosystem of suffering. Like Kid Cudi before him, 6 Dogs grew into making music for the lengthy and knotty process of overcoming. Sure, it hurts *to be*, but there has to be more to the pain than its mere existence. Sadness is not interesting on its own, and 6 Dogs was capable of so much more than dejected deliveries and penning depressing missives. His attraction to spirituality and his almost frantic desire to bore out an underlying truth in himself made his music bigger than one viral moment.

6 Dogs's success came in large part from his relatability and his likeability, but also his tenacity in playing the internet game—almost every interviewer mentions 6's buying a SoundCloud repost from iconic producer Nedarb and other emo rap collective GothBoiClique affiliates. As well, having the "Flossing" music video posted on underground hub Astari's YouTube channel was a "boost."

"[Nedarb] started showing people stuff—seriously great guy," Amick recalled. "I just kept making songs." There was a moment where celebrated emo rap producer Nedarb shared 6 Dogs's work with Lil Peep, which Amick found out about in math class. "I was super depressed, and everything [Lil Peep] said, I related to.... I talked to him a few times, I FaceTimed him once—there's like a video of him dancing to my music."

These nuggets make the 6 Dogs story so appealing; they're attainable memories. Kids in 6 Dogs's generation and the ones just below could read back his stories and imagine themselves in his position. He didn't explicitly rap, "If I can do it, you can do it," but he didn't have to—the music's sparkly humility did the talking for him. 6 Dogs didn't come up in glossy studios, primed to take over any one scene. He was an expressive kid constantly hitting a new creative apex. "I still think all my music's corny," he told No Jumper, "in comparison to what I'm making now. There's no comparison.... My new stuff, on a creative level, people aren't gonna be able to deny that I'm snapping."

The machinations of Amick's music were rife with intentionality. He was very particular with his collaborators, opting to work with friends over securing big-name co-signs. Too, he never mounted an ivory tower of pretense, for all his spiritual leaning and consideration: "A lot of the music I make, I don't really know what I'm talking about—I'm just putting it out there and leaving the dots unconnected. The people who listen connect the dots themselves."

The music Chase made was more focused on bringing people closer to themselves and each other than it was on him pontificating. He was just unassuming enough to be sincere without being questioned. Unlike Yung Lean or Peep, there was less panic about what 6 Dogs meant for the future of hip-hop. Perhaps because his come-up coincided with the fury of articles around Peep's presence in music, or perhaps, more generously, because there was no need to panic. 6 Dogs was gingerly taking over his corner of the internet and his section of the city without much ado.

"You said you loved me, no you did not," he declares on *6 Dogs'* "Chutup." The plain-stated writing and a staccato delivery helped turn these simple words into anthems of the Atlanta underground. 6 Dogs's rapping was purposefully lilted. He wouldn't attack a beat so much as he would walk alongside it as a trusted confidant, as he discovered new ways to declare the basics of heartbreak. On "Someone," Amick rolled through money and drugs before wrestling with the dehumanization of both. He was facing big existential questions in his late teens.

So much of *6 Dogs* was preoccupied with resolving contradictions. 6 Dogs dealt with the bigness of the world and his role in it by leaving his bleeding heart atop a spacey beat. The tape played out like a perpetual come-up, like the moment where you took in how vast life is, and how short, and made your peace with being who you are. But before harping on those ideas, there would be moments where 6 would pull up with a bad bitch and revel in his youth. When things came into focus on *6 Dogs*, the listener was primed to be moved, but the tape also showed Amick's age. In that way, the highs were fragile, and the low points endearing.

There are moments on the tape that don't work, especially in a jury of their peers. "Demons In The A" is outdone by "Hearse," where Amick's charm wins out over the chants that mirror the tone on "Demons." Both songs sound like mosh-pit plays, but "Hearse" adopts a more human framework, where "Demons In The A" teeters on alienating the performer from his audience. Maybe that's why 6 Dogs labeled the song "corny" in a series of interviews, because it built walls around him instead of extending a bridge. Eventually, on "Frozen Tears," he sings, "Same damn me / Same damn pain." It achieves what both "Demons" and "Hearse" attempt to do even more concisely: humanizing and demystifying suffering.

"I'm not depressed—I've just accepted the confusion at this point and it's kind of comforting," 6 Dogs mused in 2018. "Might as well do shit—I don't know what that means, but *do* shit.... It's hard to get through what I got through."

Archival footage of 6 Dogs's concerts is limited, but recordings of his 2018 concert in Atlanta following the release of "Buttcheeks" showcase the duality of being a rising internet star with music that hits the heart. When 6 Dogs hits the stage and performs with some distance from the crowd, it feels like a show dead in the water, but the moment he jumps into the pit to be with his people for "Faygo Dreams," things light up. As an outside observer, aside from his platinum-dyed hair, there's almost no identifying Amick in the mosh pit. He seamlessly blends in with the mob of kids finding themselves through his work—a testament to how powerful the 6 Dogs project was, and how emo rap is about breaking barriers between artist and listener. The footage makes clear emo rap itself is a vessel—it does what all good music does in being a golden mirror for the audience.

On October 24, 2019, 6 Dogs released *Hi-Hats & Heartaches*. Double the length of *6 Dogs*, this album was executive produced by longtime collaborator and childhood friend Pretty Pacc and was released independently after a brief stint of being signed to Benny Blanco's Mad Love. Opener "It's Worth Feeling Empty <3" was accompanied by an Astari video emphasizing how reachable Amick was, something like an even lower-budget Kid Cudi "Day 'N' Nite" video. Despite potent images of poisoned lips or dreams of whipping a 'Rari, there was a touchable element to the artist. His success was already imaginable, and his storytelling by 2019 was sharper than ever. When looking at the emo rap timeline, 6 Dogs's feels like the most natural response to Kid Cudi, built upon the soundscapes popularized by Yung Lean.

"This thing had happened in the Midwest in the stretch of 2008 to 2011, you're taking a look at musicians who were allowing people on the interior of their lives, even the less glamorous parts," author, poet, and music writer Hanif Abdurraqib says of Kid Cudi's influence. "Cudi was very touchable at that point, and you would see the interior of his life wasn't that far off from what he was expressing. It felt like a real, unbridled map of a person's life. Every corner of it. There's some reward in that. Part of this, too, is projecting one's life onto the person performing the realities of their life, to say, 'this person is not that different from me.' That level of access allows for that. It does provide a fullness of that experience; you're not just listening. It feels like you're *within* a person's life."

In much the same way Cudi was an archetype for artists in Amick's generation to model themselves after, 6 Dogs was charting a path towards being an established light with *Hi-Hats*. The unevenness of *6 Dogs* was gone as the emcee grew into his voice and the texture of his talent. *Hi-Hats* added necessary wrinkles to the 6 Dogs formula with songs like the floaty "Finger Roll (Lefty)" and lucid "Bipolar." Here was an artist who could innovate upon himself when given the space and positive influence of friends. The writing across *Hi-Hats* remained glued to familiar motifs of mental health and underground status—"the basement" was a popular locale on this record—with 6 Dogs's message hitting a new dawn on "Portals."

The playful mixed with the high-minded made 6 Dogs an enduring artist. Invoking Pokémon in the same breath as an allusion to the depth of 6's impact played out as a reminder this was just a young man enjoying his creative streak. 6 Dogs never saw himself as greater than another person; his humility continues to be celebrated by fans as they share and maintain his archives online. "Goodwill Linen" in title and form captured this spirit: "Goodwill clothes, but I'm looking elegant." The desire to flex was superseded by a need to make meaningful art.

"It's a pretty long project." 6 Dogs said on the Masked Gorilla Podcast in 2020.[4] "Me and Pretty Pacc—the legend—we made that within a month, which is really fast for me.... It's really a musical workout, to see what I could do.... The project has a pretty consistent sound, but it has to really snap. The catalyst for that was, I broke up with my girl and I had to say some stuff, bro. It was a perfect storm.... There's a few flexy songs, there's fun songs, but everything has the same underlying theme. The first track, that was the first song we made for the project— that was really soon after I broke up with my girl, moved back with my parents, and really started a recovery period. It was therapy."

Hi-Hats & Heartaches took the pained expressions on *6 Dogs* and stretched them to their limits in grim and joyful directions. Anxiety permeated this album, as well as a general wave of inspiration and conviction. Where 6 Dogs once sounded unsure of himself, on *Hi-Hats*, listeners could hear the fun behind the anguish. The album didn't approach life through rose-tinted glasses. Instead, Amick was seeing the world through "Gucci lenses" on the driver's side of a sports car. Much of the record dealt with being dumped and the betrayal of unrequited love, as on "Trust Issues." Even the clumsy lines—comparing life's choices to Netflix—are balanced nicely by the raw sincerity 6 Dogs employed on every tune.

When the angst 6 Dogs dealt in became too much for him to express, he would shelter in the typical trappings of a young artist: stacking money and securing fame. These swerves appear on almost every song and admittedly my early reading of the songs' scattershot approaches to emotions ignored the discomfort that comes with cozying up to shame.

A more generous understanding of Amick's sudden departure from his own feelings in his writing would include a nod to the intensity of emotion in your late teens and early twenties, and how overwhelming it can be to expose yourself to those nerves. This reading would explain the gentler, dreamier "Hands Up (pink sun)," which focuses on getting money for the whole gang before 6 Dogs goes to war with optimism and the "man in the mirror." 6 Dogs's knotty writing was a reflection of his own experience navigating his feelings. The flippant structure of his music presented as a feature, not a bug.

* * *

6 Dogs: I also want [*RONALD.*] to go beyond the music and I want it to be a good time. I want it to be a good time and equally be an opportunity for someone to think deeply. "When I Was A Baby," it's just fun. Babies be having fun. They be doing random stuff, but they also be thinking. It's a balancing act. I don't want to be just throwing super woke bars at people and it's like, no fun, but also you want to give people an opportunity to self-reflect. And I want to give myself an opportunity to reflect as I'm writing, because I think that's important to unlock certain parts of myself as I write and as I create a song, because I think that's a big part of it…. I like to use my music as an opportunity to affirm things and to speak things into existence, and that one's just about trying to live your best life and believing that things can go well, and taking risks based on that belief. Because I think you can make decisions based on fear or you can take risks based on faith, and there really is no in-between.

Sometimes you just got to sit back and watch things play out, and I think that's kind of where I'm at in my music career. I feel I've set up a solid foundation for a while and I've been working on myself so that I can make the best music that I can make, and really just be happy as a person, aside from the music. For a while, this music definitely saved me and definitely saved my life. I was going down a bad path and in all honesty, the music in my head, it was my last shot. I was basically, I was going to call it if it didn't work out, it was my last shot, but I knew I could do it. But I was there, I was at that point. I was there at that crossroads, and it was tough.[5]

* * *

6 Dogs's first posthumous release, *RONALD.*, arrived a few months after his sudden passing in January 2021. The album was completed and turned in before his death. Originally titled *Wave Builder's Club*, the album was meant to showcase the parallels between life and death. During promo for the album, 6 Dogs even hinted at wanting to use the album as a launchpad for a label of the same name. "Really, just fun, flex

music.... But it's more than just that," he told *Nuance*.[6] "I want to make a track that someone can turn up to, not think at all, and have a good time, or get introspective and take an inner journey, if they want to."

Dealing in those dichotomies, *RONALD.* was a record high for Chase—an album that took the push and pull of "Flossing" and "Faygo Dreams" and turned it into a soaring exercise of the value of keeping hope alive. The album is bubbly, a gentle exploration of happiness balanced by the sorrow of mental illness. Chase was onto something bigger than himself, and *RONALD.* was his chance to deliver a much grander message to his listeners. "If I'm healthy and happy, I can make a good track," he said. "Over the past year, I've tried to integrate my creative process into my daily life. I'm working on my mood and I'm trying to be comfortable and happy, because that's gonna mimic the art."

"His loss feels like a bomb exploded in our lives and hearts leaving a crater that is smoldering, gaping, and raw," 6 Dogs's family shared in a statement with *Pigeons & Planes*. "Chase was open about his mental health struggles. For the past four and a half years he contended valiantly with bipolar disorder and psychotic episodes. While he did receive treatment, these issues were at times still a struggle for Chase. The night Chase died, he took a walk and went to a building where he would watch the sunset and gaze at stars. He fell from that building and did not survive his injuries. We will never know if he meant to fall or if he was experiencing psychosis at that time. We find these unanswered questions difficult, as you probably do as well. There is no evidence that he planned his death and there was no indication given to those that were with him in the hours preceding his death that it was imminent."

RONALD. brimmed with joy—perhaps that makes 6 Dogs's passing even more painful. The confusion highlighted in his parents' statement is jarring. On the album, Chase presents with the most lucidity we'd ever hear as fans. Gone are the anxious skittering tracks, replaced by songs that feel like "sunlight medication," like that first summer sunrise waking you up and motivating you to go out and get *it. RONALD.*

displayed a dedication to healing unlike anything Chase had released prior. The album was centered around the grace and forgiveness 6 Dogs had found for himself after a period of darkness culminating in a suicide attempt. After rejecting the framework of religious teaching when he was younger, he returned to something with more gravity.

"I grew up in a religious household, and it confused me," he said in 2020. "It didn't resonate with me, it scared me. There was a lot of talk about hell and all these things. But that's not what it's about. That is so far from what it's about. Coming back and really understanding the sacrifice that, in my opinion, Jesus made, and understanding it from being an adult and understanding it from my own point of view, not what someone is force feeding me and trying to get me to believe, it was life changing, man. It was life changing and it's empowering. That's the thing with grace, it lets you step without being scared of breaking the eggshells. It lets you stomp."

RONALD. was the "stomp." On the album's rowdiest track, "Tesla Tesla," 6 Dogs left this earth in one sense, and, in another, he replayed a key line from his career: "I'm thankful for these scars." He recounted his grind and quest for success. Later, on "Time Machine," Chase reminisced once more, this time injecting colorful images of his future. The balance between past and future drove *RONALD.* The record seemed to emphasize his focus on manifestation, with each line carrying the weight of truth to come.

In the days leading up to the album's release, I connected with Chase's friend and producer Daniel Hartzog. We spoke about the making of *RONALD.*, how it was fueled by hikes and watching Pokémon. "Two friends working together, making as much music as possible," Hartzog said of the album's genesis.[7] "It was just hanging out, and it happened so naturally.... We went *everywhere*. We made this whole project together, and we submitted it together. As far as the process, we were listening to...first off, we fucking love Yung Lean. Chase loved Yung Lean so much. With this album, I got back into some older Lean, and Chase said it himself: MGMT. The sounds! The sounds on their earlier album that really made them famous, those synth sounds on 'Electric Feel' give me inspiration."

There were around twenty songs that didn't make *RONALD*. The making of "Starfire" was a turning point. As one of the final songs produced for the album, "Starfire" marked the inflection of this dance 6 Dogs was doing across *RONALD*.: meshing himself into the synths, keeping the delivery true to his past, but making sure the writing was indicative of a sterling future. "Looking at space means I'm all alone / Tears all on my phone" is decidedly 6 Dogs, but before the song drags into a "Flossing"-esque hole, the production elevates the song to something more refined. The greatest heartbreak does not appear within *RONALD*.'s content but is instead tied to the pain of watching someone blossom and shrivel due to circumstance.

"He was really proud; this album was very himself," Hartzog told me. "It reflected his carefree [spirit] going through life, and something pure." The bouncy "Beach House" acts as a nice foil to all of 6 Dogs's previous works. Made after a long hike turned into a studio lock-in, the booming bass and playful synths and lyrics full of ambition helped to turn the song into a mission statement. My early impression of *RONALD*. was that the album sounded inimitable. The productions were somehow raw and polished, and each song sounded like it spawned from the minds of the casually brilliant. For Hartzog, the results were natural.

"When you're with one of your best friends, in the studio, alone, you hit those points," Hartzog said. "I just start playing my synthesizer, and Chase would walk in. He'd go, 'Lightning and ice! Make something that sounds like lightning and ice!' And I'm like, 'Okay, dude...whatever that means.' We'd be cracking up, and I'd play a synth...I'd just play all these instruments. It was sounds Chase and I loved, and he let me be an artist on this album. He let me be my normal, weird self. The product was two people doing what they love and doing it together, fluidly."

"Time Machine" was the "lightning and ice" song. "Genie in a Bottle" was home to 6 Dogs's favorite verse of his on the album. The song is home to typical motifs of hollowness pressing up against being flush with cash, bookended by Chase's musings on healing before getting some Fendi "to wipe away my sorrow." Album opener "When I Was a Baby" was made around the same time as "Takashi Murakami," one of two songs that inspired him and Hartzog to make an album together.

The pureness of expression 6 Dogs aimed for on this album bursts out from every direction. The sound of a smashed bowl on "Tesla Tesla," the declaration of screaming on "Indigo Daydream," these minor details tell a major story of an artist who in a brief time found himself at the height of self-realization. And, as with most 2010s emo rap, there's an implied goodness to this wellspring of creativity. *RONALD.* was a rare feat—an album from the emo rap canon that showed the realities of survival. At the time of making this record, 6 Dogs was *making* it through the doldrums of his own struggles. This album captures the sound of healing, and it is a force of nature propelled by his desire to spread light wherever he could.

"We're all on this big rock together," 6 Dogs told *Pigeons*. "We are all one and the same. It's our job to, if you can, help someone else. If you can't, don't. Work on yourself, take care of yourself first, but if you can help someone else by all means do that, try that, because I think that's why we're here. I think that is our purpose. We are here to help each other and we're here to change the world. It's clutch time. There's a lot of horrible stuff going on, but there's also a lot of good people doing a lot of good things. I personally think that energy is so much stronger."

Where Are the Women?

It's a question I found myself asking near-daily as I put this book together. On every level, women with agency are essentially absent from emo rap. To write and think critically about this genre and subculture is to contend with the truth that women in emo music are used as a resource—they are the faceless subjects of screeds, the nameless muses, the derided heartbreakers and liars of the scene—and not much else. In some ways, to answer "Where are the women?" all you need to do is press play on a popular emo rap song and count down the few seconds until the enigmatic or implied "she" appears. But does "she" really appear, or is "she" merely a vehicle for the unfettered fury that so consumes this genre?

It feels almost antithetical to try and imagine a fully developed woman speaker occupying space in the emo rap pantheon. Emo rap is a definitive boys'-club production. Still, women populate the genre in a sickening way, and it is important to interrogate the legacy of emo rap as it pertains to the songs' main subjects. The writing in this music, across its twenty-plus years, is consistently disconcerting. From Atmosphere's blistering anger on *God Loves Ugly*'s "Fuck You Lucy," to the weaponization and violence baked into having complex emotions within Juice WRLD songs, the vengeful, possessive relationship towards women is potent.

To be a woman consuming and enjoying emo rap music is to be forced to compartmentalize parts of yourself. Should music force your hand, making you look away so you can tune in with relative ease? At times, I feel alienated from this music, despite being a champion of the form. At others, I feel incensed. In Jessica Hopper's *The First Collection of Criticism by a Living Female Rock Critic*, she includes her 2003 essay on emo entitled "Where The Girls Aren't" from *Punk Planet*. Hopper is scathing in her honesty about emo rock's problem, writing: "As it stands, in 2003 I simply cannot conjure the effort it takes to give a flying fuck about bands of boys yoked to their own wounding, aka the genre known as emo.... Girls in emo songs today do not have names. Women are not identified beyond their absence, their shape is drawn by the pain they've caused."[1]

Two decades on, the issue remains, poisoning new outgrowths of emo: women in emo rap do not exist beyond the crumbling imagination of young men who cannot bear to—or do not yet have the tools or capability to—stop centering themselves. At its worst, then, the culture of emo rap is the exact kind of myopic navel-gazing that even a lightly critical listener would rush to shut off when given the chance. It is easy to scan emo rap as dated in this way, challenging the conception of the melodic and ascendant music as being on the cutting edge of hip-hop in the 2010s. I am reminded of a conversation with another critic I had about emo rap's timelessness being a pain point unto itself. Hip-hop, perhaps more than any other genre, is a perfect reflection of social ideals and ills. It is the clearest of mirrors, but it is also important to note how easily rap is consequently scapegoated by majority-white critics and right-wing pundits. Despite their insistence, rap will never be the disease plaguing American people. As a genre founded on overcoming, hip-hop is most reasonably understood as a lens through which to view the pitfalls and subsequent triumphs of every walk of life in our society. Emo rap, too, is an exercise of peering into a well, looking down into a larger ailing subject: the historic devaluing of women in America.

The music, the sonic enterprise and technical advancement necessary to make emo rap achieve Diamond certifications, is so forward-thinking, and yet the content is suspended in an adolescent stasis. Part of me wonders if that arrested development is simply baked too deeply into the genre and the subsequent flow of capital. Emo rap's biggest commercial success, Lil Uzi Vert's "XO Tour Llif3," is one of its least challenging when it comes to how the woman is treated—it's one of the few songs where the speaker is a more compelling subject than any tertiary woman. "On the real, you should've never lied" feels like a slap on the wrist in comparison to other songs in the canon. The woman-as-liar is only a portion of the force propelling the song's speaker to "the edge." When Uzi sings about suicide and drug addiction, the listener sees there is more to "XO Tour Llif3" than shadowy romantic betrayal, and yet the song cannot effectively function without it. Not everyone listening can sink into the uncanny summer anthem of "All my friends are dead," but most anyone can listen to "XO Tour Llif3" and know the pain of a breakup.

There is also the unbecoming truth that the largely fictive displays of rage in emo rap have crossed over into material damage done unto women. The most visible case here is that of the late XXXTentacion, whose history of violence extends to his former girlfriend: "Discussing his ex-girlfriend, whom he believed had cheated on him, XXXTentacion can be heard saying, 'I put my source of happiness in another person, which was a mistake initially, right? But she fell through on every occasion until now. Until I started fucking her up, bruh. I started fucking her up because she made one mistake. And from there, the whole cycle went down. Now she's scared. That girl is scared for her life.'"[2] I don't mean to flatten the cycle of violence XXXTentacion was embroiled in, but even with that understanding, these recorded admissions in regards to his 2016 domestic abuse case are damning.

Naturally, I found myself wondering, "How are women even making emo rap? Are they *allowed* to? Do they *want* to?" A scan of this text would suggest they aren't—at least, not in a format for mass consumption or wider acclaim—and have no interest in doing so. The economics of music skew masculine, even for a genre that rewards hysterics and, ironically, a level of coded femininity. When a young man gets on stage and pours his heart out, we rush to assign a higher level of value to the performance if only because men in hip-hop are quietly encouraged to veil their true emotions. So, if a woman finds herself unabashedly wailing on the mic overtop a production at just the right BPM, is that emo rap? Or is it, rather, a woman feeding into age-old tropes of what it means to present her socially assigned gender role? Hysterics for some, and heroism for others.

A close-but-not-quite analog to this discussion is Maryland punk rapper Rico Nasty, whose music is more rageful than emotionally pathetic. Her 2018 single "Smack a Bitch," produced by frequent collaborator and craftsman Kenny Beats, achieved Platinum certification in December 2022. The song itself doesn't have any of the hallmarks of emo rap in the 2010s—its aggression and fuck-off attitude were much too cool for the droning cries of emo—but Rico Nasty's aesthetic flair seems to at least lightly summon some similarities. Her *Sugar Trap* series skews closer to emo rap thanks to an emphasis on Auto-Tune and drawling melodics, but still, the brimming confidence on this mixtape and the sequel has little to do with the whirring moans that made emo rap so instantly recognizable in the 2010s.

Rico Nasty is not an emo rapper in the traditional sense. She is, however, an evocative rapper taping into raw emotion. Rico's intense deliveries and her emphasis on rage chart a new course for women in rap. This is best illustrated by her 2019 collaborative mixtape with Kenny Beats, *Anger Management*. A tape meant to traverse the immediacy of anger and the process of acceptance, here we find Rico Nasty upending the need for the new class of women in hip-hop to be blustery and powerful. She invites a nuanced read of her work and position in rap's lineage. That is, Rico Nasty helps establish the presence of a woman on the mic as three-dimensional. In that same spirit, *Anger Management* imagines a future where the definition of emo rap is broadened to the point of dissolving into the North-Star truth touched on within this book's introduction: all rap is emo rap.

Despite Rico's success, there is still the question of the gentler, more immediately understood side of the genre. Where male artists in this space are rewarded for being sensitive and adopting lightly gender nonconforming fashion modes, are women granted the same opportunities to break boundaries for what it means to be emotional when there is no rage involved? The women who want to make this music are trapped in a double bind while their male counterparts can enjoy the fruits of performing a feminine affect. Even at its most sincere—there is plenty of emo rap that features artists coming to their convictions honestly—emo rap does not appear to be ready to reward a woman occupying space on her terms. The genre would have to be refashioned altogether.

As it stands, this essay is presumptuous in its own way. It assumes women want to be making emo rap as opposed to innovating their styles as artists in other, perhaps more inviting and exciting, genres. What is there to be gained from stepping into this genre? To bring women into the emo rap sphere on a mass-marketed level requires a complete reimagining of the texture and substance making up emo rap. This new world presents as exciting, with emo rap becoming brand new with the welcome addition of women molding the form.

Of course, I'm speaking in binaries here, but these thoughts also extend to nonbinary folks, trans folks, and queer folks. Does emo rap have the ability and resources to welcome a perspective outside of the largely cis male one? The commercial pull of the living and passed artists would wager no, but emo rap is relatively young. There is nothing foolish about holding out hope for the growing popularity of a new vision for the music. As with any other genre or subculture, I firmly believe the growing legacy of emo rap will only improve as the music becomes more inclusive. There are a series of untapped and ripe perspectives that would thrive within this mode. I have to believe it's only a matter of time until this daring work rises up to the surface—and that is where the women will be.

The Curious Case of Corbin

LIKE A POP-UP BOOK, EMO RAP IS POPULATED BY SURPRISES. AND there is a class of artists who, on first glance, make little sense. Their music has no business being so sticky and inventive, teetering on timeless. Paging through the canon, more often than not, you will discover a silly and curiously dressed white kid becoming a beacon of innovation. So goes the story of Minnesota artist Corbin Smidzik (known as Spooky Black during his seemingly sudden arrival in 2014), who answered the early 2010s boom of TeamSESH and BONES with a chilly, tender, and R&B-inflected single, "WITHOUT YOU."

Produced by SESH's GREAF, "WITHOUT YOU" is a melodic departure from Corbin's 2013 mixtape *Forest*, which had the then-fifteen-year-old artist emphasize his clumsier horrorcore "devil rap" chops as inspired by Lil Ugly Mane.[1] Here, Corbin brings together his base music influences—he began a musical journey on a diet of rock while learning to play guitar, and by high school he was into dubstep, emo, and singing—to produce a fully realized breakout moment.

"WITHOUT YOU" has all the hallmarks of a canonized emo rap song: pained brags, broken hearts, and looming death. But while his peers had more rough-hewn deliveries, Corbin is disarmingly adept at singing and expressing narrative tension. The song hinges on a pervasive fragility—one wrong move and it might all crumble. "WITHOUT

YOU" is soft and sheer, essentially barren, like staring into an endless, snow-dusted forest. It is exceptionally lonely. The atmosphere largely distracts from Corbin's appearance in the music video as questionable, bordering on cultural appropriation with his chain and durag. Despite his dress being little more than minstrel, "WITHOUT YOU" plays out as a deceptive earworm. It snakes and coils in all the right ways until there's a vise grip on the listener's attention. Corbin pulls off the rare trick of crafting a song that unlocks a realm of suppressed memories to stumble through.

Corbin sounds frail. His brittle but enchanting voice has nothing to do with the high-minded braggadocio of the Twin Cities hip-hop lineage cultivated by Rhymesayers. Where Atmosphere was a grimy, crunchy, and in-your-face emo display, Corbin shrinks behind his vocals. He does not adopt the density of early 2000s Midwestern rap tropes. He doesn't follow BONES and Xavier Wulf into the bloody gallows, either. Instead, he is a byproduct of the internet's flattening, reshaping, and rolling out of music culture. Ready to be picked apart by the consumer, this pastry-thin amalgam of rap and music histories is the backbone of Corbin's sound, but it also helps him unveil something new within the scope of emo rap. For as chilly as "WITHOUT YOU" sounds, it is also largely affable, thanks to Corbin's singing. In 2014, Corbin was able to unlock a strain of emo rap that draws you in, a la Kid Cudi, but shocks your system without warning.

When music critic Emma Garland remarks to me about Lil Peep's bucking traditional masculinity, and emo overall being a feminization of hardcore, I hear that in the upper register of Corbin on "WITHOUT YOU." At the time of this song's release, Corbin's doomsday vibe had yet to set in. There is merely a forlorn young man wrestling with isolation and heartache. It's not exactly the hysterical shrieking you'd expect when bringing gendered politics into play—that is, what makes something "feminine" in our national consciousness?—but you do get the impression Corbin is all but crying on the mic. Shouts are replaced with meekness.

The drawl of Corbin's voice mirrors a depressed immobilization. Listening to "WITHOUT YOU" feels like being frozen from the inside out. And yet, when the single was released, Kylie Jenner filmed herself dancing to it on Instagram. This odd endorsement sparked the song's viral ascendance—and complicated its tone. It was woeful, but it was also fit for an influencer's social media feed. It would be one of the key times in the 2010s that emo rap transitioned from digital underground spaces to the masses.

Still, press around Corbin is scarce. The artist was, and remains, reclusive. *Complex* named the song one of the best of 2014, calling Corbin an "out-of-nowhere Internet sensation" who replied to the magazine's request for an interview with a curt, "No."[2] To close 2014, Minnesota's *Star Tribune* published, "Trying to decode MN's viral sensation Spooky Black," writing, "one of the reasons it's so funny is because it wasn't intended to be funny."[3]

The article hits on the confounding nature of 2010s emo rap. Much like Yung Lean before him, Corbin drew a confused audience in with his charisma on "WITHOUT YOU." The article goes on to lightly mock Corbin's dress and his "gimmicky and dumb approach" to anonymity, between decent critiques of Spooky Black as an artist name. "I guess the joke was on me, though," veteran journalist Chris Riemenschneider writes, not finding Corbin's early offerings all that compelling or funny, "Spooky Black is proving to be more than a novelty act."

The sense of, "What do we make of this?" permeates a majority of early commentary on emo rappers' careers. Though Corbin drew less ire than Yung Lean, who drew as much hatred as *Rebirth*-era Lil Wayne, but for different reasons, Corbin's being shot down in the local paper feels like a rite of passage. Emo rap is supposed to be unnerving. If the music itself doesn't follow Atmosphere's skin-crawling presentation, then the ecosystem around the music surely will. Eventually, Corbin would grow into both his frame and his voice. He would shed the Spooky Black moniker, which was itself predated by a "Lil' Spook" alias Corbin would like to forget, and after a series of EPs, throw himself into *Mourn*, his formidable 2017 debut album.

"WITHOUT YOU" slightly revealed the paranoid depths into which Corbin was descending. "I guess it's the only kind of music I feel like I can make, there has to be some sort of dark undertone or else it seems corny to me," Corbin told *Dazed* just a few days after *Mourn* was released.[4] "I'm just, like, angry all the time about shit. I'm just not a very positive person—a lot of the time, at least. Most of the songs I wrote pretty fast, we just tried to capture moments of emotional shit."

Described as a "goth-crooner"[5] by *FADER*, the Corbin who appears on *Mourn* is positively freaked out. He dips into black metal, amps up the tension of "WITHOUT YOU," and adds a growl to his delivery that drives the album's narrative, which centers a male speaker building a bunker for himself and his partner to survive the apocalypse, culminating in two deaths and a profound sense of loneliness. Single "ICE BOY" opens the album with some of Corbin's most pained vocals. His wounded screams enhance the dreariness, and the apex line, "Don't expect to convince you to take my hand," erupts as deeply isolating.

Spanning forty minutes across ten jarring tracks, *Mourn* is a clawing plea for listeners to feel what Corbin is feeling—the dread, the deep-seated anxiety, as on "Giving Up." *Mourn* rejects accessibility in favor of discomfort. It is the underground side of what Lil Uzi Vert popularized with 2017's "XO Tour Llif3," where they brought death into the mainstream party scene with a pop filter.

Corbin rejects the tenderness of his breakout moment to make something nettling. A quick scan of the differences between *Mourn* and "WITHOUT YOU" would suggest Corbin was adopting a more traditionally masculine approach to expressing his pain. The bluntly complex emotions and the howling deliveries are gruff, but beneath lies a hysteria that scans womanly. Those crunchy breaks in his voice and the tumult of the record are not tough-guy posturing. Corbin sounds afraid. His voice has matured, but on *Mourn*, he sounds even more delicate than on "WITHOUT YOU."

"If you're looking for a silver lining in the plot, you won't find one," reads Pat Levy's *Pitchfork* review of the record.[6] "*Mourn* is a difficult album to pin down, a piece of music that is both stylistically transcendent and lyrically half-baked. Some songs find Corbin pushing his vocal chords [sic] to their limits with guttural screams so packed with emotion you can feel the veins popping out of his neck as he digs through his soul with a rusty pickaxe."

The *Pitchfork* appraisal of Corbin's often-obtuse writing follows the pattern of most reviews of emo rap citing the music as impressive and affecting, but the lyrics as confused and not quite ready for wax. *Mourn* suffers from lofty and unrealized ambitions baked into a concept album, and as a result, it is stronger as a series of vocal exercises than it is as a complete body of work. Still, the searing emotional potential was there, and by 2021 Corbin would achieve his magnum opus in *Ghost With Skin*.

Released after the majority of pantheon emo rap artists had passed away, *Ghost With Skin* is a daring entry in a withering genre. Corbin tightened up his writing, allowing it to carry *Skin* the way his singing carried *Mourn*. Now, there is balance. Opener "Tell Me" takes the wizening of a growing artist and plays out as one of the most resonant songs Corbin has ever released as he sings, "Tell me how your heart ripped open like that."

"In short, ['Tell Me' is] an attempt to give respite and consolation to someone you love, that has experienced suffering in the past," Corbin shared when the album released.[7] "An offer to be their escape. A wish to give hope for the future, and stoke their will to go on. Remaining cognizant of the realities of the world we live in, which we were brought into without our consent, but must cope and continue on in for the sake of the ones we love."

Images of caskets, endless floods of tears, and gruesome body horror sneak in between the folds of tenderness on *Ghost With Skin*. The album feels far more literary than anything Corbin had dropped prior. On "Rambo," he seeks shelter in love, but by "ctrl alt del," he delivers the best line of the record: "I'm not your bitch, I'm a person." With this open and punchy call for his humanity to be recognized at the same time as wanting to escape himself, Corbin captures the essence of emo rap. He balances the complexity of wanting to disappear but also wanting to be seen.

There is a staggering level of growth between "WITHOUT YOU" and *Ghost With Skin*, as you could expect from an artist after eight years of craftwork. Yet, it still feels luxurious to watch an emo rapper mature over nearly a decade—considering a majority of the pantheon of emo rap icons were unable to see their creativity flourish beyond a few years. In thinking critically about emo rap, some measure of prospecting is required in light of all the tragedy tainting the genre's history.

Late Georgia rapper 6 Dogs's first posthumous album *RONALD.* is a complete picture of healing and the ways in which emo rap can lead to a more holistic manner of expressing feelings, but there is no other work suggesting emo rap could mature into something healthier. Looking at Corbin, however, we witness critical developments within the scene. Corbin's transition from vibes to paranoia to some of the most raw and sincere declarations in the genre—ones that feel more complete than most other writers in the space—plays like an all-seeing artifact.

Ghost With Skin helps establish a mission statement for emo rap in a new decade. Much of what the late Lil Peep danced around in his writing was this sense of wanting to be *seen* without actually calling attention to himself. Wanting love without consequence was more Peep's mode. Corbin appears to want love as well, but in a more existential way. The music here is a lot less occupied with damning nameless and faceless women, and more concerned with the supposed interior life Corbin is battling to restore. It mirrors many of the themes of digicore, a scene that erupted following COVID lockdowns.

"I love a lot of digicore's music. Those kids are obviously directly influenced by this era of music, too," music critic Colin Joyce says. "Those kids are natural torchbearers, if not for the sound, then for the sentiments at the core of it. That's ultimately what emo rap is about: the subject matter. Kids who are alone in bedrooms and feel bad will always be there."

Even if *Ghost With Skin* doesn't follow the stylistically sawtooth tones of the subsequent digicore scene, perhaps that makes it all the more valuable as a look into what emo rap traditionalism can be in the 2020s. New artists like Dro Kenji and DC The Don adopt more rageful aesthetics, something closer to Rico Nasty than Lil Peep, but they borrow from Corbin's tortured playbook as well.

Corbin is a good barometer of emo's continued presence, with his 2020 feature on The Kid LAROI's "NOT FAIR" acting as the traditional control for a song that was obviously engineered to take over the pop arena. The juxtaposition between Corbin's vexed vocals and LAROI's sweeping choruses is a picture of emo rap's past and present. The trajectory of Corbin's career shows off the sprawl of the genre, how the fingers of the culture can spread out and clasp most anything in an ever-increasingly genre-agnostic world.

Do We Love Makonnen?

HUGELY INFLUENTIAL ATLANTA ODDBALL ILOVEMAKONNEN'S MID-2010s croon broadened the scope for emo rap artists. More than any other Southern artist of his era, from his stringy vocals to his fashion sense, Makonnen is the father of a specific branch of emo. He had an inescapable hit with the Drake-featuring, largely freestyled "Tuesday" in 2014, and, over time, became a beacon of queer rap history, despite being shunned by contemporaries in response to his coming out in early 2017.[1]

"Makonnen felt foreign, from the vulnerability in his voice, straight down to his swag," said Rodney Carmichael as he was co-hosting the celebrated *NPR Louder Than A Riot* podcast.[2] The second season of the podcast centered the double standards plaguing hip-hop's past, and how the most marginalized artists on the fringes of the genre were mistreated as a result. ILoveMakonnen's dedicated episode sought to uncover the artist's story—and draw broader conclusions about the roles queerness and fragile Black masculinity play in longstanding narratives in rap culture.

"A lot of my first, early songs were just jokes," Makonnen said. He began like all good emo rappers, producing in his bedroom, allowing his mom and first collaborator to jump on his earliest productions. As Carmichael tells it, with the way Makonnen blended pop accents and slick vocals—unheard-of arrangements that baffled even the weirdest of his peers—overtop quintessential Atlanta trap beats, he was "queering the trap." Makonnen's timbre predated the caterwauls of emo rap star Trippie Redd and swerved past the alien vocalizations of Atlanta contemporary Young Thug. Makonnen *sang* over standard trap beats from quintessential producers like Sonny Digital and Metro Boomin with his upper register squeaking down familiar drum patterns.

"Tuesday" may have been his big hit, but oft-forgotten "Sneaky Lady" stands as one of the origin points of the melodic bend of the more recognizable 2010s emo rap texture. The song is silly, discordant in a comedic way, as Makonnen sings and belts sincerely over a pure pop piano. Thematically, it works wonders. The hook is a lesson plan for emo rap writing 101. Deriding a lying woman is the basis for every essential emo rap song in the genre's canon. From Lil Uzi Vert's "XO Tour Llif3" ("On the real you should've never lied") to Lil Peep's "ghost girl" ("Tell me if you think that it's a lie, girl"), even reaching back to Atmosphere's "Fuck You Lucy" ("Interpret the eyes, read the lines on her face"), Makonnen uses "Sneaky Lady" to slot himself in wounded music history. He appears to be drawing from the bottom of the well of songwriting, and in the years to follow, Makonnen would use familiar literary signatures to anchor a wholly defining sound for underground artists in his wake.

ILoveMakonnen discovered music following the tragic loss of his best friend the day after his high school graduation. To make matters worse, Makonnen was arrested and charged with his murder: "I was in jail for about four weeks, but it was in isolation, so it seemed like forever. It was so crazy for me and my mom. It was like, the highest of our highs when I graduated, and I was supposed to go to the Air Force in twenty days. Then the day after graduation, this shit happened."[3]

In a piece for *Buzzfeed*, Makonnen shared the depth of his despair in 2008 and 2009, sitting on house arrest for two years, having his bank account drained, and falling into a series of intense suicidal ideations.

"I was just by myself, and the internet was all I had," he shared. "I had a Gateway computer at the time, and the Gateway broke 'cause it went so hard. And I had my keyboard.... I was doing music for a good year and a half online and people down here were seeing it, but they tried to say it was a meme-y thing, not really serious. There was a big war. People really hated it or they loved it, there was no in-between."

It's a common story for emo rap innovators, the polarizing opinions on their early material. As with the rise of Yung Lean, Corbin, and, eventually, Lil Peep, people struggled to tell if Makonnen was just kidding or spoiling the fabric of hip-hop—but his intensity and conviction when he sang told the full story. This *was* serious. The emotionality of his delivery speaks to the way trauma shapes the spirit. Even as he was hitting nigh-impossible high notes on "Tuesday," there was a dark richness to his croons. Ultimately, with a Drake cosign in-hand, it was easier for national critics and publications to latch onto Makonnen's music and proudly proclaim themselves fans, even if Drake remains a center point of Makonnen's rise.[4] Described by *Vulture* as a "weirdo-pop curio," "Tuesday" was named one of the 20 best songs of 2014.[5]

In 2015, Makonnen sat for an interview with *GQ*.[6] This was after the explosion of "Tuesday," well after the depression of the late 2000s. Still, Makonnen appeared humble, almost uncomfortable with the idea of fame. When asked if he was driven by ambition, Makonnen astutely replied, "No. I've accepted myself already. I accepted myself when I had that dusty-ass ankle monitor on me, and nobody gave a damn, and I wasn't singing no motherfuckin' songs. I accept my motherfuckin' self. That's what people need to start doing; but all they want to do is get accepted by everybody else."

There seemed to have been a thick boundary between the "pop curio" of Makonnen's music and his desire for the spotlight. It follows the lineage of other emo rappers who poured themselves into their music but couldn't be moved to perform the role of public figure. The clearest parallel is the late Lil Peep, whose reluctance to fame was in direct contrast with his playful and at-times boisterous early and mid-period musical output. In hindsight, Makonnen's unease with fame feels like a link to the way his perceived masculinity and sexuality were treated prior to his coming out. With that, Makonnen's December 2014 radio interview on HOT 97 with radio personality Ebro was an infamous display of homophobia and negative stereotyping.[7]

"Hip-hop's been obsessed with that," Makonnen told Carmichael of the interview, where it felt as though Ebro was trying to reel Makonnen out of the closet to push a story of queerness as weakening Black men. The artist handled the uncomfortable interaction with grace, instead pushing a message of moving past a binary of the right and wrong ways to be a Black man. Listening to the interview, there is a striking sense that rap does *not* love Makonnen—unless he conforms to damaging standards of Black masculinity. Makonnen bravely does not cower to Ebro on-air.

In the canon, most of the artists *do* perform a feminine affect—the hysterics, the wailing, the gendered color tones of bright pink—but few are treated with the same hostility and accusations as Makonnen. He represents an outlier in emo rap history, where other sensitive artists like Cudi and Peep were lambasted for the supposed poor quality of their work and the whiteness of their fanbases, Makonnen's music was more eagerly accepted, but his personhood was called into question time and time again by tastemakers. Here, the overwhelming whiteness of commercially successful emo rap presented as an unlikely shield for the likes of Peep, Lean, Corbin, and others. The sharp edge of emo rap critique for those artists rested on their whiteness and their unwelcome presence in a historically Black genre. But as Makonnen did not make coded-white music, dated views of Black masculinity were deployed in a similar way to knock him down.

The elements of Makonnen's story used against him by Ebro also acted as a saving grace, as so often is the case when artists are met with an unflattering read of their lives. "I learned everything about beauty from my mom," Makonnen recalled. "I saw a lot of caring, nurturing, loving, support." Getting into the cosmetology industry rewired the way Makonnen could express himself even before he began making music. He came into himself as a creative, and his artistic background evidences itself in his most obvious visual signatures—namely, the mannequin heads and the adept use of colors in his music videos and imagery.

By 2019, following his coming out on social media and a move to Portland, Oregon, Makonnen was back in *GQ*, this time with a more confident, but no less human, air to him. "There are other people that have pioneered and made waves for me, so that I can make waves for others," he said when asked why he balks at being called a SoundCloud rap pioneer. "I have no right to stop and say, 'Yeah, because of me, this is why all of y'all is out here doing this now.' Nah. I just want to support and bring as much new diversity of music into the mainstream, to the masses. There's no job title for that or award for that."

Despite Makonnen's influence as an artist, when the casual music fan thinks of Makonnen, they wonder about his relationship to Drake. The shaky perception of Drake and Makonnen's connection and subsequent fallout, which Makonnen attests was not about his sexuality, but about childish "old tweets," spoke to the challenge of making sensitive hip-hop.

While Drake is not exactly an emo rapper, it would be disingenuous to gloss over the way Drake's begging on the mic helped open a door for emo rap to break into mainstream hip-hop consciousness. His downtrodden loverboy aesthetic contended with the natural uncool of emo rap, and while Drake always maintained himself on the line of being stylish and a loser, Makonnen had no such qualms about softness and angst. "Mostly, he sings, and he does so in a rich, untrained, wobbly voice, with an expressive tenderness unheard of even in a rap world with Drake at its center," Jayson Greene wrote for *Pitchfork* in 2014. Drake's aesthetic may have ascended to the central point of hip-hop by 2014, but Makonnen's voice and approach altered the orbit of the genre's underground scene.

"He's become something of a cult hero for a lot of artists on the rise," Carmichael said. "The rise of the SoundCloud era, from Lil Yachty, to Trippie Redd, to 6 Dogs, to Juice WRLD. The SoundCloud era gave us more of the feels than any other.... These were artists who didn't abide by hip-hop's rules of masculinity.... One of the torchbearers was the late Lil Peep."

The very artists Makonnen inspired were the ones who most accepted him and championed his sound. "Younger artists," Makonnen told *GQ* in 2019. "When Lil Peep was alive, and also Juice WRLD. They're like, I accept you. I love your art. I respect what you do." There is a special significance here, where we can see emo rap growing up and growing out of rap's old bad habits regarding gender performance. For a subgenre so enamored with tired themes around women and their roles as dastardly muses, the genre also has a lot of heart and expands the conception of how men can present themselves. Though it feels like emo rap gives and takes with the same set of hands, the genre has the capacity to be a net positive for hip-hop's future. Even younger rising artists can look to the groundwork of Makonnen, and the brief work done by Lil Peep and Juice WRLD, and imagine a better world for themselves and their peers.

Finding Lil Peep

Gustav "Lil Peep" Åhr: Peep. My mom has been calling me Peep my whole life, that's how I got the name.... I love the Crybaby tattoo, because it means a lot to me...it keeps me grateful. People complain about a lot of shit. "Ugh, I can't get no fucking wi-fi"—shit like that. It seems very petty to me. I have good values. I don't really care about money at all, or a bunch of other shit that most people think is important.... I used to complain a lot then I kind of found myself, and [the tattoo] kind of keeps me grateful for everything that I have.... It's gonna take a while, it might even take a couple of years, but soon enough everyone's gonna get it.[1]

* * *

LIL PEEP DEFINED EMO RAP IN THE 2010S. HE GAVE THE GENRE A distinct image: pinks and purples and outlandish dress that just *felt* like the cutting edge of fashion. He injected a playfulness into his persona, despite an even more painfully diaristic approach to lyrics than anyone before him. Peep was an alchemist. He blended punk and rap with an air of nonchalance. Any classic Lil Peep song was built upon a familiar emo rock sample—those needling guitar chords that awakened memories in older fans and captured the hearts of fans Peep's age and younger.

The community of folks who were attracted to this sound could feel Peep's organic touch. Brooding accents filled out his production choices to the point where each song was a vibrant haunted house. In tandem, Peep's most emotional writing was brutally direct. He did not obscure thoughts of suicide or drug use with euphemisms. "I used to wanna kill myself / Came up, still wanna kill myself" from 2016's "OMFG" is one of the most resonant lines in the emo rap canon.

Lil Peep was born in Allentown, Pennsylvania, on November 1, 1996. According to the detailed archives posted by Peep's mother, Liza Womack, Saturdays in Allentown were spent at the local library discovering children's books. "Sometimes, a book we borrowed or bought would come with a cassette-tape version of the book, so you could listen to it in the car in addition to reading it," Womack wrote.[2] "One such book made a big impact on Gus. The book was put together from a story that Pete Seeger had told, and the story was called *Abiyoyo*. The story involves a small boy, his father, and an ogre called Abiyoyo.... Gus and Oskar [his older brother] loved to listen to it in the car. Gus's face was especially solemn and his eyes were especially wide. When the ogre gobbled up the entire sheep, the sound of Pete Seeger's voice made Gus's eyes blink. He was very quiet and listened very intently."

A fierce curiosity bubbled in Gus from a young age. Lil Peep had a penchant for expressing compassion towards himself by digging into his interior life and pulling out whatever mire laid within, lacing it with just enough evocative fiction to create something potent and timeless. He embraced the ugliest parts of life and wrote about them, even in his elementary school work in Long Beach, New York.

"In first grade the teacher gave Gus and his classmates time to write in a journal and also time to write books," Womack wrote.[3] "Gus's books show knowledge of different genres and styles.... Gus wrote a total of twenty-five books in first grade. Of these twenty-five, seven books could be best described as non-fiction. In his first five books, he taught his reader about a tree, Halloween, the world, the ocean, and bats. Later in the year he wrote non-fiction books about penguins and George Washington.... It is the fantasies that show how Gus began to play with writing. He was experimenting and playing with structure—how a story goes. He was aware of his audience and enjoyed creating a fun story to enjoy. Gus was learning how to write characters, surprise endings, and even dialog."

Going through Peep's early written material, readers discover a hugely creative and sensitive artist. Peep was in tune with emotions—his and those of his audience. His grade-school works revealed a level of compassion and care for the craft of storytelling. By sixth grade, Peep was able to write allegory and would start building the blueprint for his songwriting: "This was when Gus capitalized on his ability to communicate something without really saying it. He was expressing his feelings, his situation, and his dreams without having to tell anybody what he was really going through."

From his original—and now scrubbed from the internet—recordings as Trap Goose to his debut album, Peep's music was without pretense. It was visceral and eviscerating, but it did not come across as a series of diatribes. Peep floated above any air of severity, even in the whispers of his first songs and projects. He would freestyle rap on the back of the middle-school bus and meet with friends at the local Burger King to rap battle. Music became an even bigger staple of his life when he was living with artist Brennan Savage in the summer of 2014, after finishing high school, to attend Glendale Community College in California.

"It was completely removed from all the troubles of home, and Gus loved California," Womack shares with me. "And Emma [Gus's girlfriend] was out there, because her sister was out there." Being an out-of-state student, Gus was only able to successfully enroll in a single math class, which proved challenging, and, by mid-November of 2014, he had withdrawn. Gus lived in California with Savage, with no car, little money, and a lot of free time. Inspired by everyone from Future and Asher Roth to Speaker Knockerz and early Mac Miller, recording music became a balm for Peep's loneliness and boredom.

"'Latitude,' he made that *before* he turned eighteen," Womack says. "He's seventeen, and that's right around when he's going to one class, home alone, no car, no money. I was sending him money for food, and I think he might have been spending that food money buying pot. So, he made 'Latitude,' and that was a real song! Then he did 'Keep My Coo,' and that was maybe two weeks after he turned eighteen, in November."

"Latitude" and "Keep My Coo" were two sides of Lil Peep's burgeoning style, the former a gentle series of flexes. Peep's writing on "Latitude" was breezy, simple. He relied more on his sweet voice than on his literary merits. By contrast, "Keep My Coo" was Peep's best impression of a Xavier Wulf–styled rap performance. It had the same notes of boasting as "Latitude," and was softer still than Xavier's Memphis flows, but "Keep My Coo" presented Gus as a capable rapper for the internet age. His limited flow was cheeky at best, and overtly rough at its lowest point on the song's bridge. Yet, it was mesmerizing. Prescient comments on the official "Keep My Coo" video see fans referring to Peep as a "young legend."

"Gus came home early, at Christmas," Womack remembers. "Then, he went back to California, and then I had three missed calls from him, 'I gotta get out of here.' So, we sat and I'm talking to him and I'm on the JetBlue website. He came home Super Bowl Sunday, February 1, 2015."

Once home, Gus continued making music and shooting videos—something that felt close to his family history as his grandfather played multiple instruments, wrote, and constantly videotaped Peep and his older brother, Oskar. These early recordings—"feelz" from 2015—had an air of giddiness to them. The lo-fi video for "feelz" was shot in the basement of Gus's childhood home, a 1920s Spanish-style construction that was potentially haunted, as he'd express on "toxic city." The "partly truth, partly fiction" nature of Peep's writing, paired with his already immense charm, helped make it enchanting. Lil Peep's music did the important work of creating a dedicated space to honor emotions no matter how distressing. He was the architect of a vast room for fans to come in as they wished and experience life's difficulties with someone who promised to understand in as few words as possible.

"A lot of great writers, over time, are able to write with that kind of economy," critic Colin Joyce shares. "You're just saying the thing, you're not dressing it up. Very plainly, boldly saying how you feel... there's a risk in doing that. He acknowledged it—there's a risk of coming off as a crybaby. There's a risk of people dismissing your experience, but for him it was so honest. That's what makes great writing for me, in general."

Most importantly, Peep never tried to impart meaning onto the listener. There was a respect paid to the fan, allowing them to design their own meaning independent of Peep's intent. Where so many emo rappers could be described as mirrors for fans, this music felt even more active and engaging. Peep's work is visceral— beguiling in the same way a massive fire hypnotizes despite the destruction it is causing.

"My first reaction wasn't all positive, and that was true to a lot of people as he was reaching beyond SoundCloud," Joyce continues. "There's something that was gut-level revolting at first. It was so— and remained throughout his career—unvarnished. He sings and raps in metaphors, but he was very transparent with his emotions. He was thinking about existence in a direct and uncomfortable way. He was looking you straight in the eyes and telling you he wanted to kill himself. It's hard to listen to music like that. It was hard to see the art in it, at first. But then, the more and more I listened to it, I realized that *was* the art in it. That is a big part of what ultimately drew me to his music. I could hear in those early songs he had the making of pop music greatness. You can hear that from the very beginning."

Peep began to break out nationally in 2016 with a pair of mixtapes—*crybaby* and *HELLBOY*—yet critics jabbed at his music, calling it "stupid as shit."[4] The fans didn't care. They saw the somber angst of suburban malaise in Peep. They saw themselves. "He was great for the same reason his music put people off," Joyce wrote in 2019.[5] "It wasn't just that it was sad or dark or depressing, but that it was all of those things without apology or pretense. He never pretended that things were going to be ok, or that there was a greener pasture that he could see on the other side. He embraced the darkness, luxuriated in it."

"It connected instantly, and when I was reading that *Pitchfork* profile that called him the 'Future of Emo....' It was interesting, but as a journalist, I was more interested in the way he was upsetting people," music critic Emma Garland recalls. "As a music fan, I didn't care. This is really fucking good! I wasn't thinking about what it meant. [The early criticism] says more about men and masculinity than anything about the artist. The vast majority of criticism or mockery that I saw of him came from men. That's been the case for any iteration of emo. It's always men being presented with a different way of being male, and I find it interesting to see them try to reconcile that for themselves. I don't think he deserved it, but I expected it."

Like so many artists in the 2010s, Peep's career was accelerated by the internet. By 2017, he would be a star with glossy productions and a studio album that would help him tour overseas and achieve international acclaim. Before the universal boom of "Awful Things" from *Come Over When You're Sober, Pt. 1*, there was a smattering of projects that charted Peep's growth and an increasing confidence in his own voice. Reaching back to his first full-length releases from 2015, *Feelz* and *LiL PEEP; PART ONE*, the music had a quietly solemn touch. Whispering in his bedroom, these songs ached with loneliness, like a wounded outcast's pleas to be understood.

"Peep pioneered music for a lot of kids," rapper midwxst shares. "There weren't really artists who were talking about this as teenagers, living the shit that we were going through. Understanding it, as teenagers. Talking about drugs, being lonely, feeling unwelcome, not feeling like yourself. All of those things—we didn't have artists we could identify with and look up to."

"Thinking back to interviewing him, one of the things we talked about is his music being born from a profound loneliness," Joyce says. "Growing up in the suburbs and just feeling completely isolated—his music captured that feeling in a really deep way."

Part of the appeal of Peep's music, and the resonance, came from the way it was created. In 2015, Peep had three pieces of gear: a mic, Beats headphones from a Best Buy near his childhood home, and a laptop his mother gifted him as a high school graduation present. This humble setup carried his early defining works and made him all the more touchable as an artist. "Gus was pleased with what he was able to accomplish on his own, and decided to release *Feelz* in May, 2015 via his own SoundCloud account and via BandCamp," Womack wrote.[6] "*Feelz* was the first release Gus uploaded for the public—and kept uploaded for anyone to listen to. It was the first music he made at home in Long Beach. *Feelz* represents the beginning of Gus's commitment to writing lyrics and making songs full time."

Feelz was home to three tracks, each of which helped establish a pillar of Peep's musical sensibilities. "Toxic city" was rife with the subtle elegance that would mark later songs like "benz truck" and "Problems" from his first studio album. "Feelz," with its at times humorous writing, revealed the personality beneath the darkness of the music. And the centerpiece, "life," telegraphed every deep hit Peep would have in the few years to come. "Life" tackled the nuanced complexity of being a person with blunt writing.

Made during Peep's late teens, these turbulent emotions knot together into a touching offering. *Feelz* presents Peep before his voice would rise up in the mix, before the wails and blaring guitars. Music that is closer to BONES—TeamSESH has production credits on *Feelz* and Peep credits them as a major influence—than it is to Peep's ultimately grandiose and pop-aspiring sound.

"His way of singing, and the way his voice sounds and his use of melody, it's probably more than any other emo rapper influenced by pop punk and the noughties," Garland notes.

"He gives you a *feeling*," Womack agrees. She also shares that Peep was hugely influenced by the punk bands introduced to him by his brother. He paired that music with being the quiet observer of the family. "'Toxic city' is so...I *love* that! 'Life in the background, up and down a mountain.' I know he and his brother, and his father, went to climb Mt. Katahdin. And 'life in the background,' he was in the background of his relationship with his brother and father. He was one who watched and noticed certain things.

"And then, in 'toxic city,' 'Shawty say my house is haunted / I say I don't give a fuck.' Gus said to me, 'Emma thinks our house is haunted.' We moved to that house in May 2012. I didn't know Emma existed until a friend told me, 'I think I saw a blonde come out of Gus's window.' She had been climbing in and out of the window for I don't know how long! So, that line is a true thing. There are these true things that, if you know him, you know that little piece is real. But the whole *feeling*, it doesn't matter if things are true or not."

The tones on "life" and "toxic city" bled nicely into Lil Peep's most affecting song, "Star Shopping." Composed in August 2015, and released the following day, this song was the ultimate tether between Peep and his growing fanbase. "Look at the sky tonight, all of them stars have a reason" became a calling card for Peep, who would perform portions of "Star Shopping" a capella at concerts to add to the gut punch of lines like, "I know that I'm not that important to you, but to me, girl, you're so much more than gorgeous," and "This music's the only thing keeping the peace when I'm falling to pieces." Here, and perhaps for the first time, allegory was replaced with direct imagery. "Star Shopping" was a beating, bleeding heart of a song that helped fans relate to Peep, and then wrap that emotion back inwards.

"With 'Star Shopping,' I sent [the beat] to him," producer Kryptik said.[7] "I was getting fifty plays on my songs, dude.... I didn't think anything of it. When I made 'Star Shopping,' I was proud of the beat. It was the first beat I tried to make for somebody. I made it for him." Kryptik continued on to explain that the artist who was sampled on the song, Yppah, and his record label, reached out and the song was eventually removed from streaming platforms. "Yppah basically said, 'If Peep wants to keep it up, he has to pay.' So, when you see Peep performing the a capella, I'm pretty sure he's not legally allowed to perform 'Star Shopping' because of the record label. But he still did it anyway, which, I support him. I'd probably do the same damn thing."

Crybaby was made in a handful of days with a similarly humble set up as *Feelz*. "He did the first six tracks in Pasadena," Womack shared with *Masked Gorilla*.[8] "Four tracks in Long Beach-slash-Island Park... June 9 he flew back [to California]...then he dropped it the next day, June 10." Talent and rigor go hand-in-hand. His prolific nature, and the sheer speed at which Gus could make a song, aligned with this essential artist's truth: mistakes are corrected with subsequent efforts. With that, *crybaby* built upon the affecting tones of "Star Shopping" and "life." The familiar samples on *crybaby* made key songs feel like they had always existed despite being birthed in quick succession in Long Beach. On the tape, Peep appeared to be an excavator of latent emotional truth.

"One of the first things I heard about Lil Peep was that he sampled Brand New [on 'crybaby'], and I was super impressed by that," writer Danielle Chelosky shares. "Who expects a Brand New sample and then someone rapping over it!" In 2021, *Alt Press* shined a light on Peep's sample usage, connecting him to the indie and punk scenes: "From the early days of his career, his songs featured a diverse array of scene-bred samples mixed with trap beats and loaded with lyrics that solidified him as a genre-melding force."[9]

"If you weren't able to place the samples themselves, you probably still had the associations of them," Joyce adds. "You may not know who Pierce The Veil is, but you still know, 'oh, this sounds like what my friends' angsty bands sound like around town.' It gave a different frame of reference to everything he was going for."

Crybaby works well beyond the sampling Peep employed to ground listeners in his influences. The tape is bare, raw, twitching in ways that are unnerving. Closing track "driveway" uses images of guns and shooting himself to an emotional end. For the first time in Peep's career, he was able to tap into the zen of releasing himself in service of his work. "lil jeep," where Peep's directness is matched with veiled specificity ("I see your face when I look out the window"), revealed a sensitive and meticulous young man vying to be heard, but perhaps fearful of being perceived in full. In mixing reality with fiction, but with no clear line between the two, Lil Peep was a writer's writer with a keen sense of how much of himself to give and how much to chalk up to being an artist.

"His delivery and the distance in his delivery is such an interesting contrast to the way he writes, too," Joyce explains. "He is spilling himself out, but he's floating above it in the way that he sings and raps. 'I feel horrible, but that's just how it is. This is just what life is like.' That's what so many people connected to. His whole public persona is an invitation to people who felt the same as him. Shit's bad, but that's just how it is for everybody. It's a gesture of a lot of emo music. You want to relate to the person at the heart of the song, but aesthetically and in his voice, there was a way of relating that was distinct from his peers."

Perhaps more groundbreaking than *crybaby*, though, was the subsequent *HELLBOY* project, "his most iconic tape," as producer Nedarb declared.[10] The tape was also Garland's entry point to Lil Peep, and she describes the early impressions as an "immediate attraction." *HELLBOY* was recorded between July 31 and September 19, 2016, and released a week later on September 25. This speed was not uncommon for Peep;

he was keen on gutting himself daily, letting whatever messy expressions tumble out of him and using them to ascend a spire of potential.

"It's funny because every time we made a song with him, it was really *fast*," producer Yung Cortex explained. "We had made ['hellboy'] in like a day, pretty much. Peep told me and [producer smokeasac] to finish the beat, so we finished and sent it to him, and he was just sitting there on the couch with his headphones on, pretty much what he did with any song. Then, an hour later, he went and just recorded something real quick. He'd do it extremely fast and quietly, and then he'd have a whole song done."

HELLBOY was fearsome and intense. A lot of the playfulness of earlier records was shredded and thrown aside, replaced by powerful displays of disconcerting emotion. Here is where his writing truly shined. Peep took a bludgeon to complete sentences, turned them into tortured fragments, and shipped them off to keep himself steady. On "OMFG," Peep detailed wanting to kill himself no matter his circumstances with a piercing economy of language. The song was recorded during a party with Peep "singing his heart out," as Nedarb remembered, in the middle of a shared loft in Los Angeles.

"It feels very unfiltered and natural," Garland says in regards to Peep's writing. "He says what he needs to say, in the way he needs to say it. He's not *trying* to be poetic, it's more so, 'Oh, fuck. I miss this girl who had a fat ass.' It's very base, but then if you combine that with the way he sings, he weaves these melodies, screams, and yelps, and that hits for me the most. It feels very unforced, and I just *believe* it."

In 2018, *Pitchfork* heralded *HELLBOY* as the "masterpiece of Lil Peep's lifetime."[11] In 2022, the review's author, Matthew Strauss, says, "I still think that. I do think he found his footing with *Hellboy* in a way he hadn't found previously, and showed potential, but wasn't able to [reach it]. What I'm attracted to with *Hellboy*, in particular, is the hedonism, for lack of a better word. It's the rawest of his work, as far as being pretty lacerating to himself and others. It's mixed super loudly and he's giving it his all, as if it's the only time he's going to. That's what keeps it as his canonical work, for me.

"There's an attractiveness to that emotional honesty and being that open in songwriting. That's what a lot of people seek as listeners: I wanna hear what this person is actually feeling. I'm listening to them for a reason. It has a directness, perhaps, that emo previously had in a different way. But I think he unlocked a system that works, of getting rhythmic and melodic parts, and singing very emotionally on top of them."

In February 2017, though, Peep outdid himself once again with one of his most iconic tracks, "witchblades" with Lil Tracy. This was the perfect distillation of everything Peep got right in his music: the chanting chorus, the dark and drug-laced imagery, and the subtle goofiness that takes just enough of the edge off. Garland describes "witchblades" as the most effective Lil Peep song: "That's what made a lot of people pay attention. It's something people could get behind, and it encapsulated almost like a meme version of what he's all about. It's a very neat summary of the whole Gothboiclique agenda."

Lil Peep's first studio album, *Come Over When You're Sober, Pt. 1*, arrived in August 2017. The record's seven songs, according to Garland, seemed to reach the "final form" of the breakout tapes. The album reached for big choruses over sweeping guitar riffs and ditched the rough-hewn edges of the mixtapes for glossy finishes that centered Peep's voice and aesthetic more than ever. "In terms of the artist that he was becoming, it was the starting point of what was going to come," Garland says. "What was going on for him around that time as well, aesthetically and visually, that album is really his peak."

The crown jewel came with the massive pop crossover single, "Awful Things." Recorded in November of 2016 and released in late July 2017, it is the most grandiose piece of music Lil Peep released. "For him, he had some sort of pop ambition," Joyce says. "'Awful Things,' that is a stadium-sized emotion. He was making music that was meant to feel like even if you're in the rafter seats, he's talking directly to you. That is affecting in its own right." "Awful Things" had a lot of the great qualities of "witchblades," and of "Star Shopping" and "life" before it. In contrast to those early breakout moments, though, there was something even more fulfilling about singing along to "Awful Things," about belting, "Bother me, tell me awful things." It felt like the anthem of a generation, written with supreme concision and delivered with a twisting vocal melody.

While "Awful Things" reached for pop stardom, other songs on the album revealed Peep perfecting his more ominous sensibilities. "Benz truck" and "Problems," the bookends of the album, played with pained purplish chords and sounded heftier than any of the other doomsday records Peep had released. "Save That Shit" featured the most satisfying flex of his career: "Nothin' like them other motherfuckers / I can make you rich."

"The true tragedy of Lil Peep as a listener is that, to me, it felt like he was about to become the biggest thing in the world," Joyce says. "I buy into his whole thing that he was trying to help people who felt like shit. Even though his music was maybe an over-the-top version of emotion, at least in terms of how I experience emotion, it still was affecting. If he was making a version of that music that could reach more people, as in 'Awful Things,' there's a lot of power to it."

Peep did not live to see the vast impact he had on the music industry—his life was cut short on November 15, 2017, just days after his twenty-first birthday, due to an accidental overdose of fentanyl-laced Xanax. The night of his death, there were videos of his body shutting down on his tour bus posted to social media. It was impossible to stomach.

When thinking of his legacy, Peep's fingerprints appear all over new and tired acts alike. "I certainly don't think that mainstream pop or rap would look the same without him," Garland says. "I don't think we'd have Machine Gun Kelly doing what he's doing without Peep. Absolutely not. For better or worse."

The cult acclaim, certainly on the cusp of sustained mainstream success, didn't entirely mesh with the softness of Peep's interior life. "Having met him and interviewed him, and having seen him perform, he really shrinks behind his music," Garland remarks. "He really shrinks behind fame. It seemed very reluctant—he wants to do music for a living but didn't want any of the repercussions that came about. I always think his artistry, in the sense of his actual essence...I absolutely think that's at odds with the vehicle of emo rap, with the energy of the shows and the intense fandom. The noise around the whole thing just seemed very at odds with him as a person. That's my impression. It might be projection, but it felt like there was a real split."

Peep's quiet charm did not always jibe seamlessly with the enormous attention he was receiving. "I'm not sure music is what Gus wanted for his life, because he was so young and got swept up in this," Womack says. "He was *good* at it, but he was also doing a job with touring. He was, as you can imagine, somebody who felt uncomfortable. He was never out, and liked to have his room full of all his friends. He talked quietly and didn't yell. He came home again in the summer of 2017—he'd been in England—he asked if he could come home to New York. It was right after his friend had a seizure and Gus called me, completely freaked out. He just wanted to come home.

"He was furious, when I finally got him home, because of the snafu of the release of *Come Over When You're Sober*. He had not been allowed to release it for months. He always just made something and released it—then the album leaked. He was furious, and then the people he was working for, they said he couldn't have fire in the 'Awful Things' video. He was fed up. He didn't want to do more music. He said, 'I'll just do fashion, or design clothes. I don't want to be Lil Peep anymore. I'm done.' He was just twenty! I don't think we could say music was what he wanted to do."

Losing Lil Peep was painful. In the five-plus years since his untimely passing, there have been a bevy of online fan pages dedicated to Peep's legacy. The collective mourning around Peep has evolved into a consistent and mindful adoration. These folks come together to celebrate Peep's life and his impact through anniversary posts, studio photos, emotional outcries missing his presence, and historical recountings of his music and videos. Every detail of his legacy, as upheld by these online spaces, feels precious.

"The community matters so much to me, because I'm so proud of him for what he's done," Womack concludes, through tears. "There's a thread of what people say, which is he's able to express for them things they haven't even thought of, that they felt. He's expressed that feeling for them...and allowed them to find their own feelings. That's what the youth are saying to me. The older people, in their forties or fifties, they appreciate that same quality, because they're also appreciating that their kids are sharing that with them. It's giving them an avenue to communicate with their children.

"My therapist recommended a book called *When Your Child Dies*. Nobody should ever have to read a book called that, but it is very, very good. So, I say to people, 'When your child dies, you die, too.' The person who you were is now gone. There's another version of you and you're living in a nightmare. But you get used to it. I'm lucky in that you don't want your child to die, so you're going to hang on to every single thing. So, all the people who know, at least, that there is a person named Gus Åhr, it helps. I'm very grateful—it keeps him alive."

Lil Uzi Vert's "XO Tour Llif3"
Codified Misery in the Mainstream

PHILADELPHIA RAPPER LIL UZI VERT ATTEMPTS TO GRAB FIRE WITH their bare hands.[1] They freestyle their music off the top of their head, letting a sporadic delight light up their every song. The artist's ascendance began in 2015 with a series of colorful and playfully explosive mixtapes. The at-times cacophonous sound would later be understood as a harbinger of rage rap, and many acts would follow Uzi down the experimental fox hole they had burrowed, building out a network of artists and a culture of throwing elbows at even the glossiest of shows. Uzi's career ultimately unfolded in fits and spurts in the late 2010s and early 2020s. In 2017, though, they were the single hottest performer—the artist who seemed best positioned to unseat Drake as the most-talked-about rapper. Uzi's jittery and exciting presence was inescapable. Uzi was up next, and it's true they became a Grammy-nominated, bona fide star, but in the sphere of emo rap, their contributions were even more gargantuan.

Emo rap firmly became a recognized mainstream phenomenon in 2017 thanks to "XO Tour Llif3." Officially released in March of that year, by May the song would crack the Billboard Hot 100's top ten and achieve Platinum RIAA certification. Before 2017 ended, the single would be certified Platinum five times. Recorded while Uzi was on tour with R&B's crooning obsession The Weeknd, the song uncovered the tangles of emo within even the coolest of acts. As one of the late 2010s' hottest exports, the drones and full-on angst of "XO Tour Llif3" upend the idea of emo rap as the splicing of lameness with the inherent flyness of hip-hop. There is no shortage of cool in the song's DNA. "I know Uzi wanna go to the clubs," 808 Mafia producer TM88 shared with *Genius* about the making of the song.[2] The beat was crafted in a pack of twenty, without knowledge of what Uzi would do once they heard the production. TM88's mindfulness of club BPMs solidifies the backbone of "XO Tour Llif3" being a traveling hit. It was engineered to move people, and the song did just that, codifying the sound of abject misery in the mainstream.

Throwing a dart at the lyrics sheet yields striking results for a song that went on to be a club staple. But this is what the people wanted, especially with the latest political turmoil in America. "It's odd to hear everyone in the club shouting along to Uzi's alternately slurred and wailed cries about depression, Xanax abuse, suicidal thoughts, and dead friends. And yet here we are," *Billboard* noted when the song was named their fifth best of 2017.[3] Odd, yes, but also incredibly compelling. The country was stressed out, the people with the money, the people with time to enjoy music—hell, even the people with little of either who chanced into the song—were instinctively looking for something pretty *and* gruesome. And Uzi delivered.

"I do think that 'XO Tour Llif3' is one of the most significant songs to come out in that whole era," critic Paul Thompson affirms. "I was in Vegas with a friend in the summer of '18 and in the middle of the day, we were at a pool with a DJ. You would see these monied people in their thirties partying, and they were screaming along to 'XO Tour Llif3.' I remember both of us being like, 'This is really, really dark.' It's weird that this is not a cult song—it's weird that this is a plausible number-one hit, and it's the closest to a big suicidal pop hit in years."

"XO Tour Llif3" is a nettling masterpiece. When Uzi sings, "I might blow my brain out," there is less of an insistence that heartbreak and subsequent suicidal thoughts are the *fault* of Uzi's ex. Rather, the perfect storm of Xanax addiction ("I'm committed, not addicted, but it keep control of me") and detachment from reality leave the speaker on the first verse meditating on taking a gun to his temple. This horrific image makes the second hook ("Push me to the edge, all my friends are dead") appear like a dejected threat. Does it matter if Uzi lives or dies after experiencing such suffering when crippling loss only distorts and displaces any signs of hope? Does hope even exist when Xanax fails to mask the pain? Lil Uzi Vert poses this existential question over a bass-heavy beat the country was singing along to for months—and now, years.

This dichotomy is significant. The disconcerting mainstream success of "XO Tour Llif3" calls to mind Atmosphere's car-crash aesthetic on *God Loves Ugly*. Where rapper Slug was wading through a self-inflicted muck and mire, Uzi absconds the slimy textures of emo rap's past to deliver something a little more polished, but no less fraught. That is, in the earliest days of emo rap, there was a sense of shamelessness and nakedness, matched by the lo-fi nature of the music. Atmosphere's work was an irresistible series of personal tragedies—no one could look away, and the unease of sinking into the music was integral to the experience.

By contrast, "XO Tour Llif3" is easy to love. The sounds are trendy and captivating. Uzi works with as much bare intensity as Slug, but because of the soundscapes, it's only *after* we are sucked in that we realize we're in a pit of drama. As the single unspools beautiful, brutal nightmares, it's clear "XO Tour Llif3" landed at just the right time. Much like Kid Cudi's "Day 'n' Nite" captured the isolation of the internet in the late 2000s, Uzi managed to speak for a nation of bugged-out people perpetually on the precipice of crisis, hiding behind glitz with a fear of being seen for who they really are.

The writing and production are just a piece of why "XO Tour Llif3" rang off so immediately. It's also the *way* Uzi sings that makes the music near universal in its ability to connect with listeners. "It's the whiny, pop-punkish delivery of the choicest lines that helped make the song a crossover pop hit," Joe Coscarelli wrote for *The New York Times* in 2017.[4] Where the late emo rap icon Lil Peep used samples to bring prospective fans into his world, Uzi's familiar droning—the way they yelped and pitched their voice in that "pop-punkish" effortlessness—helped make "XO Tour Llif3" feel familiar. The kids who grew up on Warped Tour were unknowingly ready for the next generation of artists to hit that raw nerve with their vocals. Uzi's impish delivery bent time and brought everyone together, from thirty-year-olds on stimulants to lonesome kids in their bedrooms ready to scream.

In her 2018 *New Yorker* recap of "the Year in Sad Rap," writer Carrie Battan remarked, "When the song was released, at the beginning of the year, it felt like a revelation: an ode to depression that also got people moving at night clubs."[5] This was the song you danced to, to forget. It was an escape for everyone aged thirteen to one hundred. But there was more to the song than emo posturing. "XO Tour Llif3" had roots in a painful reality, and perhaps the realism propelling the song was the reason it landed in every corner of music, with pop and rap fans uniting under the common need to get wasted and wish for death under the flashing lights of a dance floor.

Looking back, "XO Tour Llif3" felt like one of the last times that the hip-hop monoculture had a consensus hit, and it was an unbelievably sad one. In May 2017, *Vulture* ran "Lil Uzi Vert Has a Modern-Day 'Smells Like Teen Spirit' on His Hands,'" in which writer Frank Guan wrote, "['All my friends are dead'] wouldn't sound out of place on an emo chorus—in fact, it's a perfect emo chorus—but it takes on new color and depth in a rap context because it isn't just a metaphor.... By applying the operatic death-courting and death-defying postures of Dashboard Confessional or Marilyn Manson or Smashing Pumpkins to his own lived experience, he's created a genuinely new version of the hip-hop elegy."[6]

Guan is spot on. Emo rock often employs banal writing, to the end that being dumped can only be so traumatic. On "XO Tour Llif3," death is far from figurative. We are dealing with real loss, real addiction, and nearly insurmountable trauma. It is overwhelming—or it would be if that pain wasn't also the catchy anchor inspiring online dance challenges.[7] The way consumers took to Uzi's obvious hurt scans as appropriative, but also expected.

"XO Tour Llif3" presents a reality where the jokey qualities of emo can be read alongside the tough nature of some of hip-hop's most resonant moments. It helps to see Lil Uzi Vert is at least somewhat in on the emotional upheaval of their work. Uzi's coy shoulder shimmy in the video for "XO Tour Llif3" brims with unexpected snark. The contrast between death and danceability is jarring, but it also speaks to the direction our culture was heading. In the mid-2020s, gallows humor has become the de facto coping mechanism of the younger generations.

It makes sense to see artists following Uzi's rise being encouraged to bring their wounded experience into the pop arena in order to sell records. It's not a novel enterprise, but this formula feels uniquely suited to our current American moment. Take a series of unspeakably dark memories, blend them with relatable and crumbly vocals—the kind anyone with a mic can at least attempt to imitate—throw them atop a carefully crafted 808 line, and you've got emo rap magic.

The critical praise for "XO Tour Llif3" was aplenty, and the labels were further tuned in to the financial viability of emo rap, especially after their ears were perked up by the boom of SoundCloud hits from rappers XXXTentacion and Trippie Redd. Soon began a scouring of the digital underground for the next "XO Tour Llif3." According to Thompson, this was just a function of economics. "When SoundCloud became an obvious system for major labels, and when streaming became a source of revenue for artists on a sub-major level, when the numbers proved this was viable, people were not gonna make music that was as obscure." In the months following "XO Tour Llif3," a host of artists bubbling online—the aforementioned Trippie Redd, Lil Peep, XXXTentacion—all released commercial debuts. As the years drew on, more emo-skewed rap artists secured major label deals: 24kGoldn, iann dior, and Australian Juice WRLD protege-turned-pop-hitmaker The Kid LAROI.

These artists continued to fly closer to the pop song sun. 24k and iann dior's 2020 No. 1 hit "Mood" borrowed heavily from the "XO Tour Llif3" playbook with just the right twists—neutering the suicidal motifs and replacing the brooding beat with a lighter guitar riff—to craft a catchy tune about toxic romance. LAROI managed to do the same with his emo-inspired, but clearly pop-minded, project *F*CK LOVE* in 2021, having the album hit No. 1 on the *Billboard* 200 over a year after release. These new mainstream misery anthems ("Mood," LAROI's "Go") are far more palatable displays of desperation.

"XO Tour Llif3" represents a peak for emo rap in the larger music culture conversation. After hitting such a gory apex, the genre course-corrected to be more accessible. In the post–"XO Tour Llif3" world, death is out on the charts, and yet the backbone of emo vocal delivery remains. The new crop of emo rap hits may be subdued, abandoning the gothic tones of emo rap from the early 2010s, but they represent an important piece of the lineage nonetheless.

These new hits show off the function of commerciality, sanding down a genre to bring it to even more audiences. The rawness of the SoundCloud era could only make so much money. After emo rap bashed into the "XO Tour Llif3" ceiling, it was time for the majors to adapt the culture for even more profits. When "Mood" plays at a coffee shop, I wonder if emo rap has achieved the goal of all music executives: to have their product exist in all spaces for all people. More generously, perhaps these days—in a new era, where COVID-19 has changed our relationship to life and death, both abstracting death in mass numbers and making it extremely personal—the people making this music are ready to be a little less depressed.

Raider Klan, SoundCloud, and GothBoiClique Gave Emo Rap Community

EMO RAP THRIVES IN THE MISUNDERSTOOD CREVICES OCCUPIED BY wounded young artists. But that is not to say the foundational acts existed in vacuums or ran like lone wolves. Key collectives predated by, or featuring members from, Florida's Raider Klan group—Schemaposse, Hollow Squad, and TeamSESH together as SESHOLLOWATERBOYZ, Thraxxhouse, GothBoiClique—saw essential artists band together and forge their own paths in the music industry. At the same time, they organically redefined the look and feel of emo rap in the 2010s.

These groups presented emo rap as resilient. Before the majors realized the genre was commercially viable thanks to 2010s hits from Trippie Redd, Lil Uzi Vert, and Juice WRLD, emo rappers were given only crumbs of industry help. In part, this became an essential ingredient of emo, with artists carving out their own lanes outside the mainstream. Many key artists, like BONES and Xavier Wulf, are regarded as independent hip-hop heroes, showcasing the value of owning your creativity and operating with an almost delusional level of self-belief.

Tracing the knotty history of late 2000s and 2010s emo rap collectives reveals how these groups splintered and poured into each other over a short span of time. The bursts of energy driving these sometimes thirty-plus groups bubbled over into equally important offshoots. The genesis of nearly every current and former collective can be traced to the SpaceGhostPurrp-founded Raider Klan. Kicked off in 2008, in Carol City, Florida, Raider Klan was originally home to underground rappers Xavier Wulf and Chris Travis, among many others, who went on to have their own careers within Schemaposse, TeamSESH, and Thraxxhouse in Seattle.

In the sprawl of the ever-evolving internet, before the most recent online-scene gold rush, these collectives were essential to giving emo rap a home base, with Raider Klan serving as a God particle for much of the harsher emo rap that took over by the time XXXTentacion rose to prominence in the mid-2010s.

SpaceGhostPurrp's prolific, gothic, and blustery catalog does not necessarily define emo rap in the way Xavier Wulf and BONES's works do, but his unabashed dedication to craft and the creeping sensation of listening to his howls speaks to the fundamentals of the genre. Purrp's work has less to do with a tortured soul and more to do with syrupy and tortured production. His work—despite an ultimately fraught relationship—with A$AP Rocky and the A$AP Mob is critical to his influence on artists like Yung Lean and 6 Dogs, who grew up on the drawling Southern roots of Purrp's sound. SpaceGhostPurrp's oeuvre charts a course for emo rap to become stylish; Purrp's ear for production helped bring swagger to the emo rap acts he inspired. At the same time Kid Cudi was making it acceptable to be lonely in skinny jeans, Purrp was laying the groundwork for emo rap–adjacent artists to inject an undeniable cool into their soundscapes in the 2010s. A majority of this work found its way to SoundCloud.

In addition to SpaceGhostPurrp, several Raider Klan artists and affiliates were SoundCloud pioneers. While so much of emo rap is classified as SoundCloud rap, not all SoundCloud rap is classified as emo rap, and as we've entered the 2020s, the platform's aesthetic has shifted from the aggression of Raider Klan et al. to a digitized, controlled chaos as evidenced by the digicore subculture so many other platforms and tastemakers tried, and failed, to commodify. In the 2010s, SoundCloud was a revelation for our rough-hewn emo rap genre. Emo rap, at its best, is raw and intentionally unpolished, reflecting the lack of material resources and DIY spirit of the culture.

The ability to upload directly to SoundCloud and share music without major label backing or a distribution deal democratized music and created a new space for emo rap to thrive. The direct-to-consumer approach of SoundCloud allowed for any stress of perfectionism to melt away. That is, these songs still felt perfect to their creators and audiences, but they didn't need to be traditionally, technically, bulletproof. The wonkier the mix, the better the music felt—without the gloss of a big studio budget, emo rap on SoundCloud felt scaldingly pure.

"Me, Bones, and Xavier created that little SoundCloud shit," former Raider Klan member and successful solo, sometimes-punk rapper Denzel Curry said in 2018. "We set the tone for everybody else, and then they just took it a bit further. We definitely brought the audience to SoundCloud.... When I think of SoundCloud, I think of distorted bass and weird ambient-type sounds. Hard-ass beats and a lot of melody. I really have been doing all of that since Raider Klan. Raider Klan was crazy because we all had our own personalities and our own little worlds when it came down to this music. It was the first step to creating your own weird little universe. Everyone was attracted to that."[1]

As artists found their fan bases online, the music improved—effort in, quality out—and there was a mutual sense of growth established between the rapper and the listener. A fan had the opportunity to grow alongside their newfound favorite acts, and the speed at which most emo rappers recorded and released meant there was endless potential to revel in the minute tweaks from song to song. The intense workmanship of these artists, and the artists in the emo rap orbit, was perfectly timed with the changing technology in the music industry.

As on-demand streaming grew to dictate the way music is packaged and released, in a more-is-more model, emo rap felt uniquely poised to succeed. Streaming changed the user behavior of the casual and dedicated music fan, making them insatiable in response to the sheer volume of music available. Since real-time confessions are a key tenet of the genre, there were no growing pains. Emo rappers were ahead of the streaming curve.

SoundCloud, combined with social networks, allowed for emo rap collectives and solo artists to prosper from their bedrooms. Be it Kid Cudi's capturing the stark loneliness of the MySpace era or groups forming on a blogging site like Tumblr, the digital age reshaped the way emo rap was made and distributed—while keeping things decidedly DIY. The GothBoiClique (GBC) collective recalls the way Atmosphere worked the indie touring circuit back in the 2000s.

GBC was a safe space for young men to express themselves and experiment with their music, taking the fringes of emo rap and making them the norm. The group was created to delve into the mire of adolescent angst. The ten members, Wicca Phase Springs Eternal, Cold Hart, Horse Head, fish narc, Yawns, JPDreamthug, Mackned, døves, Lil Tracy, and Lil Peep, took their witch house and rock roots and rewrote the emo rap playbook one whine at a time. There's also a slew of affiliates like Drippin So Pretty and yunggoth, especially with the latter's breakout track "Idk How to Kill Myself," who were essential to building the GBC sound.

GBC was founded somewhere around 2012 by Wicca Phase, whose DIY musical lineage originates most notably with his band, Tigers Jaw. "Trying to give a potted history of Gothboiclique is as hazy as trying to explain how your friendship group came together," music journalist Emma Garland wrote in 2018.[2] GBC's name derives from a beat Cold Hart had sent Wicca Phase, who himself began the Wicca Phase project via Tumblr. The original goal was to build a collaborative network that poured into itself with compassion and creativity.

"There's a whole book that could be written about how things came together, but I'll give you the short version," fish narc shared back in 2020.[3] "I participated in a DIY culture in Seattle, and it was based on alternative spaces that were almost always all-ages—precursors to what people now call safe spaces—with leftist politics and inclusive goals. That's what I grew up in; I went to college in the Northwest and saw that culture decline. I played in bands, booked shows. In this moment that I felt it was declining, I was aware of, and a fan of the music of, Raider Klan and Lil Ugly Mane and Black Kray."

"It's important to note Mackned was experimenting with Witch House-influenced production and experimental vocals and was also making trap, and he grew up in Seattle listening to grunge," fish narc said. "Wicca Phase's background was in Tigers Jaw and his penchant [was] for boppier bass. Cold Hart has this penchant for doo-wop and '50s rock, but he also was making Chicago-influenced music. Horse Head.... We played in bands before all this happened. We played shows together back in 2011."

Coming from different states and with different tonalities, there are myriad reasons why GBC should not have been able to work. And given their knotty history, the collective *doesn't* always work. But GBC is bigger than the sum of its parts. They are easy to identify with—a point of pride almost to the end of rooting for a sports team, and picking a favorite player, and setting up camp for life. The collective's appeal is as much about the music as it is about the representation of intense and heavy emotion by way of a strong logo, style of dress, and each member's easily recognizable music signatures. In the early and mid-2010s, a GBC song was a thing in flux. You could turn to the auto-tuned moans of a Lil Tracy, the hyper-serious punk-trap exercises of Wicca Phase, or to the looser early raps from Cold Hart, whose 2022 album was released on punk label Epitaph, and still discover a strong through line of emotionality and camaraderie among the members.

Wicca Phase Springs Eternal's 2023 self-titled album, boasting his strongest writing to date, also feels like an inflection point for a post–Lil Peep emo landscape. "Twilight Miracle" sounds like a song birthing itself as the "light through the trees" silhouettes any dirges that marked Wicca Phase's music prior. Across the record, Wicca Phase Springs Eternal dances with fire, battles emotional consequence, travels through mysterious portals, and flirts with occult imagery. This album has sprigs of lightness. His voice is subsumed by notes of New Wave in the production. The result is a modern-day answer to *Through Being Cool* by Saves the Day, how the gentle whimpering marking each song replicates a house-party-reject singalong.

GBC also established a visual language across its members in the same way BONES became known for compromised VHS effects. From the early lo-fi videos from Lil Peep and Lil Tracy—where "witchblades" is the essential GBC image—to the most polished Cold Hart videos, there is a humility to the Gothboi presence. These videos continue to recall the meat of the blog era, where the YouTube numbers would be driven by images of aspiring artists palling around with their best friends. For as depressing as the lyrics could be on any given GBC-affiliated track, the imagery always included a layer of fun.

There was the sense, in the flesh, that these artists were *enjoying* themselves. The hope was not in the dour production or the constant invocations of death and doom, but rather, packed into the jeering smiles and playful appearances of each of the GothBoiClique members. Isolated, Lil Peep singing, "When I die, bury me with all my ice on," is pretty sad, but in the "witchblades" video, he is giddy, showing off said slight ice and writhing around in a cramped room. The live performance footage, too, speaks to the team-like essence of the collective, with hordes of people on stage at any given time, regardless of who was performing.

Still, GBC was not without its own pains. There was, perhaps media- and management-fueled, infighting. "I just feel like people don't respect the relationship we had," Tracy said when asked if he was written out of Peep's history. More materially, multiple members have struggled with drug abuse. Lil Tracy brushed with death after a drug-induced heart attack.[4] He was also committed to a psychiatric ward following troubling social media posts.[5] Amidst all this pain, particularly in Tracy's life, the writing surrounding GBC was focused on recovery. Headlines positioned the artists as survivors of their own personal hells, fastidiously claiming these acts cannot be erased.

GothBoiClique's DIY spirit brings to mind the late-2000s rise of Kid Cudi and "Day 'n' Nite." Much like Cudi captured and utilized the droning agony of the bloghouse era to his advantage, making the unnerving depression of social networking a facet of his rise, Goth-BoiClique represents the boundless nature of digital connection in the 2010s. "It's crazy because some of these clothes and sounds that we have started—other kids are making them now and it's popular," Cold Hart told *Clash* in 2021.[6]

Here were ten young men who could turn to each other to harness and nurture a wildfire of creativity. In some respects, GBC represented the best the internet had to offer artists: easy access to a like-minded and supportive community. With that, GBC, like Raider Klan and TeamSESH before and concurrent with them, were able to quickly and efficiently brand a strain of emo rap in every facet imaginable, from fashion to sonics. At present, more than anything, GBC is a springboard for growth. As Cold Hart described: "I don't think I would ever go back to it, because we started as teens and I was just hopeless.... I've been going back to my old stuff, like really old stuff. And it's kind of embarrassing to listen to, but it also just inspires me because I just hear what my sound was building up to."

As the GothBoiClique members continue to evolve their individual sounds, their early works still have an outsized influence on artists rising through the newest layers of the digital underground. In 2022, rising artist and producer blackwinterwells, who toured with fish narc that summer, told me they began singing because of Lil Peep: "It's important that people understand this project started because I like Lil Peep and emo rap. It's not rock, but that's what I draw from."[7] Though Cold Hart has the sense fans and other artists regard Peep as "king," all of GBC is, at least in part, responsible for the pop-punk resurgence in mainstream music culture following the COVID-19 pandemic lockdowns. It just goes to show: if you leave enough creatives to stow away in their rooms with nothing else to do but wallow, the natural inclination towards emo will bubble up and fester. Or, more plainly, as Lil Peep sang on 2017's "Avoid": "GothBoi, I'm the one you can't avoid."

Trippie Redd Gets Dubbed
Emo Rap's Sinatra

Trippie Redd: There was a lot of people, and they gave mixed opinions about my music coming up. I never took it like "I was trash," I just looked at it like people [perhaps] didn't understand it, yet. So, It was up to me to make them understand it—which made me strive even harder. I wanted to make people understand my music, what I was doing and how I was doing it. People are ultimately subjected to their own opinion and can say what they want, but I wanted to try and prove people wrong. I wanted people to like my shit. It makes me feel competitive, it makes me work hard and amaze people.[1]

* * *

FOR MAJOR LABELS, THE SOUNDCLOUD RAP GOLD RUSH BEGAN IN the mid-2010s, thanks in part to Trippie Redd's genre-shifting 2016 single, "Love Scars." In tandem with Lil Uzi Vert's "XO Tour Llif3" bringing emo rap misery into the mainstream, the Canton, Ohio-born Trippie Redd tipped off executives to the power and profitability of emo rap, and ensured Redd would become one of its faces. In his childhood home on 14th Street, which he commemorated with a face tattoo, Trippie grew up on a steady diet of Lil Wayne, 2Pac, Andre 3000, and Drake—basically anyone with lyrical chops who could also imbue melody and, eventually, Auto-Tune into their work. He recorded his first song, "Manu Ginobili," at fourteen. "It was like, 'black diamonds and my gold Rollie, ball hard like Manu Ginobili, I ain't got time for no fake or phony....' I was just freestyling."[2]

Freestyling full songs, a 2010s emo rap technical mainstay, would quickly become the modus operandi for Trippie Redd. "Love Scars" was laid down in a single take in a dark room, "on some screamo shit." The single's piercing vocals and Trippie's penchant for hitting evocative high notes helped elevate the tune in a sea of artists flooding Sound-Cloud with emo rap attempts. Paired with painfully direct writing, "Love Scars" laid the foundation for late 2010's emo rap to become more than a batch of suddenly charting singles.

"Trippie Redd helped define the genre," *Pitchfork*'s Matthew Strauss says. "At the time, for work, we were listening to Zane Lowe's Apple Music show every day. He would play Trippie Redd all the time, and his first breakout song ['Love Scars']. That probably did a good deal of familiarizing people with young Black men singing about heartbreak and anguish in a way that perhaps they hadn't."

"You used to say you in love" Trippie wails on both verses. As the song progresses, he sounds like he's being ripped open by grief and rage. His sound goes beyond pain to something more slippery and gruesome. Unlike other emo rappers in his class, Trippie was baking in writing he deemed "really savage," representing the boiling over of feeling that comes with heartbreak. Some of the writing on "Love Scars" is gross, akin to Atmosphere's *God Loves Ugly* ("quit stepping in my cum"). The song blitzes by in under three minutes, at times exceptionally disorienting because of the haphazard vocal layering. But when the production accents fall away and Trippie's voice cuts through, there's a bluesy twang to his otherwise gummy delivery. These competing textures make "Love Scars" thrilling. The biting tension of the melody and Trippie's slip into bombastic rapping on the second verse would become a hallmark of his biggest songs.

Some of Trippie's earliest music to bubble up in his hometown leaned closer to the drill music of the Midwest—he cites "Angry Vibes" as a launch pad for himself in Canton—than the heartfelt angst of his most popular records. In 2017, when he caught national attention with "Love Scars," writers didn't know what to make of him. This was the late 2010s, "XO Tour Llif3" had been out for a couple of months, and emo rap was on the verge of becoming the next industry cash cow. It seemed natural to compare Trippie to Uzi, at the very least their dots on the emo rap timeline share a lot of space.

At the same time, the moral panic over hip-hop's future was once again called into question as young artists invoked more rock elements and unexpected melodies, and fewer breakbeats. Terms like "mumble rap" and "SoundCloud rapper" rose to prominence as ways to dismiss the music from the new generation. Even the most celebratory of Trippie Redd commentary would rely on comparison and dismissiveness—"Trippie Redd Is on the Way to Becoming Soundcloud Rap's Frank Sinatra" was one particularly catching headline from 2017, as if to suggest emo rap couldn't stand on its own or was somehow unworthy.

"They always compare me to Uzi," Trippie Redd shared with *XXL*.[3] "I try to explain how it's not Uzi. It's like we low-key kind of have the same cadence, but not... [Uzi's] just now making a song that relates to his life like that. That 'XO Tour Llif3' shit, that's why it went platinum. He finally figured out what he needed to do.... Okay. I been doing that type of shit." In other interviews, Trippie Redd gets downright adversarial when asked how he feels about comparisons to other artists. He prides himself on his versatility and authenticity, wishing to touch as many genres and moods as possible while maintaining his artistic core.

Though Trippie's breakthrough record was recorded in Columbus, Ohio—along with a string of now-deleted singles that helped Redd find his sound—he equally credits his time in Atlanta as helping him launch his career, paired with an emphasis on stripping persona. "That's how I really went viral: just being me.... There's no character," he told *Pigeons & Planes*.[4] This mentality aligns strongly with the continued rise of social media as a means of eradicating the gap between artist and listener. The music puts fans in the tortured mind of an artist, sure, but nothing complements that effect better than also being privy to their minute-to-minute, largely mundane, thoughts. This unshackled experience feeds back into the music, creating a cycle that lets fans feel as though they really know the interior life of their favorite artists. Trippie Redd's gut-level freedom on wax is porous. Listeners can open themselves to his music in much the same way making the music flays open Trippie.

Critical reception to the *A Love Letter To You* tape was lukewarm in the few reviews that popped up online.[5] As with most emo rap criticism, the prevailing theme revolved around the perceived immaturity of the writing and song structure. A compendium of listener reviews ranged from trashing the record for a "whiny" quality in his voice, while others praised Trippie's "raw" textures.[6] It's difficult to parse whether the feelings listeners had towards Trippie's initial offering were an appraisal of his specific music, or working towards a bigger rejection of emo rap and using the tape as a vehicle to express their disdain for the subgenre. It calls to mind the early 2000s work of fellow Ohio native Kid Cudi, whose loner croons laid much of the foundation for Trippie Redd to develop the rageful emo rap sound alongside counterparts in the South Florida rap scene.

To this day, discourse around the quality of Kid Cudi's debut mixtape and debut album feels flippant. On the tenth anniversary of *Man On The Moon*, *Stereogum*'s coverage of the project moved between validating the "first-thought-best-thought venting" of the album and hammering the notion that the album was nothing more than "catnip for late '00s blog omnivores and lonely stoners alike."[7] The piece interrogates the merit of intimate fan connection as it concerns the effect and legacy of music, ultimately landing on the generous claim that "Kid Cudi's debut may not be the most revelatory album ever made, but its success has allowed hip-hop to cover musically exciting and emotionally important territory over the past decade.... The world is a better place for it."

What Cudi cracked open in terms of emotionality, Trippie vaporized with anger. But on *A Love Letter To You*, there's a tension between the versatility Redd wants to employ—"Romeo & Juliet" and "It Takes Time" are tender in contrast to "Love Scars" and "Blade Of Woe"—and his ability to uncover and lean into the sound that distinguishes him in a wave of artists borrowing from Kid Cudi's lexicon. On "Can You Rap Like Me?," Trippie throws everything we've known of him in the mainstream consciousness away and brings us back to his Lil Wayne influence. It's a confusing but exciting apex—here's a rapper's rapper *choosing* to warble and wail. The presence of this song, especially with its classic production, draws a solid line to the hour-long Juice WRLD freestyles to come. In the same way "Love Scars" continued to open up the rap world to this new flavor of emo rap, "Can You Rap Like Me?" was enlightening and affirming—these kids weren't eschewing hip-hop's roots. They were watering them.

The *A Love Letter To You* series spans five projects, with the second installment releasing in October of 2017. Before the year ended, however, Trippie would release his second and most mainstream breakout record, "Dark Knight Dummo" with Travis Scott. The Platinum-certified single teased his 2018 debut studio album, *Life's A Trip*, and was a departure from the pained emo rap that helped Trippie catch fire. "Dark Knight Dummo" was more interested in flashing wealth ("My diamonds dancing hopscotch, they holding hands") than recounting the scorn of a broken heart. Like the swerve of "Can You Rap Like Me?," "Dark Knight Dummo" revealed another side of Redd—he had the capacity to make ballistic trap bangers with as much ease as heartfelt trap ballads. Additionally, securing a Travis Scott co-sign when Scott's stock was rising in a post-*Rodeo* and *Birds in the Trap Sing McKnight* world added gasoline to Redd's rise.

The beat for "Dark Knight Dummo" was made by Honorable C.N.O.T.E. prior to him ever hearing Trippie Redd. The producer eventually heard "In Too Deep" while in a Los Angeles studio with Dallas rapper Fooly Faime, who had been advocating for Redd and his music. Instantly, there was a connection. "He got a voice like a '90s rock singer but he can rap too. That's a crazy combination," C.N.O.T.E. shared following the song's release and subsequent charting on the *Billboard* Hot 100.[8]

"Dark Knight Dummo" features Trippie's immediately recognizable screeching wails. The raps are steady, but it's the long notes that make this song a cultural pillar. On the hook, Trippie's voice stretches beyond imagination—it sounds like a cat fight. His calling card, the fluidity of his singing, takes listeners to a precipice—will Trippie's voice break or won't it? While there is always the opportunity for these textures to hew too close to a gnawing whine, the critical and fan praise for the song proves Redd stuck the landing.

By June 2018, before releasing his debut album that August, Trippie would be named an *XXL* Freshman, a coveted title since 2008 for any emerging rapper. By the 2010s, several articles popped up assessing the importance of the *XXL* designation. In 2012, the *Village Voice* published an honest look at why the Freshman list was a cultural moment, despite questioning a number of the selections.[9]

"The predictive value of the list hasn't improved since, with abundant misses (2009's Charles Hamilton and Cory Gunz, 2010's OJ da Juiceman and Pill, 2011's Lil Twist and Fred tha Godson), premature calls (B.o.B was a freshman in 2009, but blew up in 2010; Curren$y and Wale showed up on 2009's list, and Big Sean and J. Cole got the look in 2010, but none of the three found their niches until 2011), and just a few right name, right time selections (Kid Cudi in 2009, Meek Mill and Kendrick Lamar in 2011)," Andy Hutchins wrote. "But that doesn't make it a bad list, or a bad exercise; it just makes it Sisyphean."

Four covers later, in 2016, hip-hop critic Yoh Phillips wrote, "Time and time again, year after year, I've noticed the perception that being an XXL Freshman has the ability to blow an artist up, potentially changing their career. It's a mentality that you can associate with the rap blogosphere—if I can get my song posted on this one site or do an interview with this one publication, the results will be life-altering. Even deeper than blogs, we all look for that shortcut that will change our lives with the wave of a magic wand. Sadly, it rarely happens that way."[10]

Between these two quotes lives an ocean of similar sentiments across personal blogs and digital publications. The question, by the time Trippie Redd's class was selected, became: "Do rappers need *XXL*, or does *XXL* need rappers?" On the 2018 cover, it seemed the magazine had the answer. "The class with clout," read the headline, a clear nod to the awesome wave of internet stardom that overtook hip-hop as SoundCloud became a home base for the underground scene, and an additional admittance that *XXL*'s status as tastemakers was being dwarfed by the DIY spirit of these young artists.[11]

In his video interview with the publication, he was deemed "Rap's New Rock Star,"[12] "I love Kurt Cobain, my favorite band is KISS," Trippie told *XXL*. Later features would adopt the rock-star tone as well, fueled by Trippie's desire to "relay the message" of rock music's Black roots and vocal freedom. Though his sonics were further from the guitar-led moments that categorized Lil Wayne's *Rebirth* era, Trippie Redd feels like a natural outgrowth of Wayne's modeling what a rap rock star could look and act like. Both artists share a similar irreverence and emphasis on prolific output. Both artists are touchpoints in understanding the development of emo rap. It also helps that Trippie Redd has many of the visual signatures Wayne popularized pre- and post-*Rebirth*, while maintaining his own gothic flair. The video for "Dark

Knight Dummo," for instance, features Trippie blasting handguns at a zombie invasion.

Despite being cagey in early interviews, Trippie Redd grew into his stardom with grace. In 2021, *Bleu Magazine* published "The Unorthodox Life of Rap's Most Notorious Rock Star, Trippie Redd,"[13] which aimed to humanize him. Trippie spoke to the gun violence permeating his life, even before his music career. He expounded on the value of life and expressing love whenever possible. Spliced between commentary on his infatuation with numerology and his tattoos, there are a few nuggets that see Trippie Redd wizening. As one of the few remaining artists from the SoundCloud emo rap boom of the mid-2010s, Trippie's maturation is an exciting prospect, if only because the fans of this genre have few options for music to grow alongside them.

Trippie Redd is an exemplar of the blemishes making the music feel *real*. There is a limit to a listener's ability to connect to an artist if they present as too perfect. Trippie's presence on wax and on social media is fallible. He revels in the imperfections of his increasingly tinny voice. The tears and fractures of his singing reveal his humanity and give his work a unique character. In a genre largely defined by a feeling rather than a strict structure, Redd's ability to stand out from the first needle drop is golden. There is no mistaking one of his songs for a contemporary's.

And though Trippie hates the comparison, much like Lil Uzi Vert's "XO Tour Llif3" proved the financial viability of emo rap, Redd's career highs cemented the longevity of the quintessential "SoundCloud rapper." Be it circumstance—Trippie is a small member of a surviving class—or his sticky sound, there is much to glean from the way Redd has endured even in the face of critical pans and a changing tide in emo rap.

What to Make of XXXTentacion?

MY INTRODUCTION TO XXXTENTACION CAME MILLING ABOUT A concert venue in New York. The DJ was playing the hugely popular "Look At Me!" while a swarm of kids made their best attempts at moshing. Intrigued, I searched up the song and discovered a "graphic testimony" from a victim of domestic abuse.[1] Suddenly, the dissonance was staggering, watching people throw around their bodies with reckless abandon while I was processing how a young artist could do something so heinous. This was merely a glimpse of the XXXTentacion question. As X's short career was taking shape, he transformed into a vehicle for critical discourse on music consumption and ethical responsibility.

XXXTentacion was the most serious and severe emo rap practitioner to rise up from the 2010s SoundCloud boom. His style was gutsy and wounded. He was a proficient musician who drew a massive and loyal fanbase: a sea of kids who hung onto his every word, for better or worse. Caught in a deep cycle of violence, the young artist's presence in hip-hop raised a series of ethical questions as court records revealed a disturbing history of physical abuse—his controversial persona and insistence on outbursts also did him few favors with critics.[2] He was named an *XXL* Freshman, and national music outlets began to pen nuanced pieces detailing the ins and outs of enjoying his music in spite of the violence he had perpetrated.[3]

Born in Plantation, Florida, and raised in Broward County, XXXTentacion had a tumultuous upbringing. In a 2016 interview with *No Jumper*, the artist born Jahseh Onfroy details a fraught childhood: he was kicked out of schools, engaged in a lot of fighting, and had hardships with his mother that led to Onfroy resorting to brutal violence at a grade-school age. He expressed empathy towards her situation, and the challenges she faced attempting to raise him, though they warped him as a kid. "I chased her," he said. "I used to beat n****s at school, just to hear my mom yell at me or talk to me... I just wanted some attention."[4] In these early moments of his *No Jumper* interview, there is something deeply sad about the way Onfroy framed his young life through violence as the only means to achieving emotional fulfillment.

"When I first found out about X, it was not because of his music," shares journalist, cultural critic, and on-air correspondent Ivie Ani. "It was because of reports of all his legal troubles. I didn't know about his music—an introduction like that, through the consumption of the reporting on him and social media... That was a lot of people's introduction, especially people not in his age group. It was the perfect storm."

Before his tragic murder in June 2018, XXXTentacion was positioning himself as repentant. The timeline between the flurry of reporting on his transgressions and his redemption tour was brief, cut shorter still by his death. X was only twenty at the time. Fans—listeners, the crew of artists he ran with, and the young artists he's since influenced—were heartbroken to have lost their idol before the public could see the new leaf he was turning.[5] After his passing, in an article about his memorial, *The New York Times* described him as "a messianic youth-culture figure."[6]

"I was inspired by the change of heart and progress in life by X," young emo rapper midwxst emphatically shares. "If X could flip his entire life around, flip the way he went about things, and the way he reciprocated emotions. He worked towards all those things—they didn't just come overnight. Not a lot of people can get to that status among the kids, especially kids my age." Midwxst is not alone—the conception of X as redeemed over a long stretch of time is a common thought in his fan community. When thinking or talking about X with people who feel the music as a part of their identity, time seems to become brittle and break away. The deep attachment to his work overwhelms the harsh realities plaguing his legacy, and yet, it still doesn't feel right to adorn XXXTentacion with the "monster" label and wash our hands of the conversation.

XXXTentacion's success shocked the industry, led by this fervent fanbase. X began both of his studio albums with opening "instructions," a warning shot of sorts that was meant to weed out those he deemed unable to open their minds to his music and ultimately, to his own mind. He sought loyalty from his fans, making sure to differentiate between diehards and casual listeners. "If you're a fan, you abide by everything I believe in," he told *No Jumper*. "I have a cult fanbase—I speak to my fans; I help my fans."

"I think he needed his fans," music journalist and *Look At Me!: The XXXTentacion Story* author Jonathan Reiss explained.[7] "I think he had a deep void in his soul—he was one of those people who was always trying to build a family, and I think he did that with his many fans. Something that's not really written about is the fact that he communicated with fans directly throughout his career. He really built those relationships in a way that I don't think anyone else has in this era. I think it was of a function of the fact that he genuinely needed it."

Look At Me! details the challenges X faced: lack of parental guidance, potential mental disturbances, allusions to psychosis, poverty, traumatic loss, and more, without absolving X of his actions. The opening set piece, explaining the physical hole in Jahseh's heart, matches Reiss's larger, more philosophical look into X's need for family. An undercurrent of X's loneliness drives *Look At Me!*'s reporting. Graphic portraits of the wounds X caused color the biography, but so do the many fan and artist tributes. It becomes difficult to square the incredible sensitivity and impact of his music with his unscrupulous behavior. At times, *Look At Me!* struggles to pin X down, refusing to label him as purely a monster or a musical visionary.

The book is one of the more nuanced takes on XXXTentacion's life and art, an attempt to provide balance during an era of media sensationalism. To close the work, Reiss writes, "XXXTentacion's story was a hard one to tell. His acts of violence were too numerous and gruesome to ignore or downplay.... Just as his violent behavior cannot be denied, the brilliance of his work cannot be ignored."

Brushing off XXXTentacion grew more and more difficult as his star rose. His breakout moment, December 2015's "Look At Me!," was an aggressive and fleet-footed beacon of South Florida's hip-hop sphere. Unlike the luxe sounds coming from the Rick Ross port of Miami, the South Florida rap scene was much more intense and ghastly, almost repulsive. Young artists would go ballistic on the mic and ship their works off to SoundCloud. The South Florida hip-hop boom that encompassed everyone from X to Ski Mask the Slump God, to Denzel Curry, to Kodak Black was sudden. As X's music evolved from his scattershot mixtapes and Members Only crew compilations to the sonically rich sound of his debut album, *17*, his streak of violence and incarceration followed. Much of *17* was written while X was in jail, with some of his drawings from that time adorning the album cover.

17 appeared as an outlier for X's sound, playing as far more R&B-focused and more traditionally emo than preceding tapes, namely *Revenge*. Though X's content had always had shades of anguish, *17* was the first time he fully embraced the form of emo rap. The album was tender. The productions were soft, and the suicidal writing was evocative. There was a constant throb of pain, an overwhelming loneliness lacing X's every breath. His voice, in this gentler soundscape, was arresting. X was often regarded as brightly charismatic by his peers, but his earliest offerings were missing that tug of personality. *17*, a record whose heart was cold-blooded depression, made X relatable. In the same way young kids flocked to Juice WRLD and Lil Peep, they could now see themselves in X. The music had gone from taking over Southern Florida to being a national phenomenon. *17* reached No. 2 on the Billboard album charts.

Mainstream reviews were less than flattering, all at one point centering the moral question of listening to XXXTentacion in light of his domestic violence case. *Pitchfork* wrestled with the question of essential music and the difficulty of taking part in X's orbit.[8] Writer Meaghan Garvey described *17* as "a collection of shell-shocked bedroom R&B and hopeless, rock-bottom grunge that deals exclusively with depression, heartbreak, and suicide." And it is true the album is incredibly proficient. Smaller blogs and college papers covered *17* with more of an appetite than national publications, and the more niche the audience online, the louder and more heaping the praise for X's versatility.

Despite X's unfavorable online reviews from big league outlets, during his time in jail and once he was released in March 2017, X's every move was publicized as a means of taking a moral position on abuse. There is a note in *Look At Me!* about the Streisand Effect, and the relationship negative, and even finger-wagging press, has on the rising stars of the internet age. The question of the press's role in developing a star is limiting, however. A better question is that of the music critic as an arbiter, and of the capacity society has for accountability, rehabilitation, and reintegration.

"Two things can be true at once without absolving an artist of their transgressions," Ani explains when I ask her how she squares XXXTentacion's fans attesting he saved their lives with his music. "It's honest to say that someone's music or cultural production has had some semblance of value to whatever fanbase and music canon, whilst that person was committing crimes and being who they are. Those things are true!"

"I also think people aren't thinking critically about the psychological element of how we view celebrities," she adds. "That's the missing piece of the conversation of separating the artist from the art, or not. A couple years ago, I interviewed a psychologist to help explain why we mourn celebrities and a big reason for that is empathy. Empathy is more of a subconscious thing—it was very enlightening, because that strong emotional response completely influences the way we engage with their work. Empathy makes us feel like we can connect with these people, when they have even just *one* similarity with our lives."

To think about XXXTentacion is to consider the systems and cycles of violence in America, how they permeate the lives of young people and produce outcomes like X's life and tragic death. "To only be twenty and develop into such a violent person, it says more about the environment and systems that created a young person like this than it does about the short amount of time he had to enact this violence," Ani agrees. "He's not the only person, and he won't be the last."

As Reiss details in his book, and as X himself details in his early *No Jumper* interview, his harsh—to put it lightly—upbringing is just as much responsible for his violent inclinations as X himself. It would be disingenuous to suggest XXXTentacion was born a perpetrator of evil and lived out a self-fulfilling prophecy. The deeply rooted issues at play, which evidence themselves in his crimes and his music and persona, are just as important to critically consider.

Had XXXTentacion not been brutally murdered in broad daylight, with the video of his death promptly viewable on social media, I do believe by 2023 critics and fans would have been able to have more robust conversations surrounding his work. Moreover, it has been documented that when writers attempt to have these conversations—particularly Black women writing from the perspective of survivors—they are attacked and endangered by X's fans. To suggest a fanbase is the direct responsibility of the artist is foolish, but it is valuable to note those fans are an impressionable group of kids who fed off of X's own crass energy. At the very least, the fan response to any nega-tive remarks on X's behavior can be seen as a mirror into the persona the artist cultivated.

And yet, most of the critical writing on XXXTentacion following his death has an empathy-filled hole. "If we see a video of XXX getting shot, everything goes out the window," Ani says. "It's clear that some people are letting the video of XXX being violently killed eclipse his violence. But the natural, human response is empathy. It's an automatic response our brain has. And imagine how much less control a child or a teenager has with that feeling. This is why the younger demographic is not able to separate that art from the artist."

XXXTentacion's fans stood their ground on a bedrock of some of the most important music in the emo rap canon. *17*'s "Jocelyn Flores" is regarded by Internet Money founder and producer Taz Taylor as one of the best emo rap songs ever made: "All the shit happening with X, you're getting a look into his mind. You feel how he feels." *17* followed this ethos, with each song appearing as a blitz of gushing depression. No song touched three minutes, and the album itself barely crossed the twenty-minute mark. It revealed X as an extremely efficient writer and performer—he needed only a few seconds to worm his way into his listener. It's almost parasitic, except there's a real relationship built between X and his fans, who see him as nothing short of a giver.

By 2018's *?*, X had become the de facto face of emo rap's musical prowess and deep-seated controversy. And still, the album was a bub-bling example of the breadth of XXXTentacion's capabilities. Following the spoken opening manifesto, "ALONE, PART 3" played like a mum-bled emo rock demo from the middle of the country. Even the more rap-minded tracks, "Moonlight" and "infinity," had the spiritual and mentally disconcerting undercurrents that helped define X's sound. *?* hinged on XXXTentacion's biggest crossover hit, lead single "SAD!", which was posthumously RIAA-certified Diamond. Unlike the snarling "Look At Me!", "SAD!" is a strictly suicidal and tender pop smash. It could only exist in a post–"XO Tour Llif3" world, where Lil Uzi Vert broke open the doors for miserable rap music to topple the charts. Though "SAD!" would not reach the chart heights of "XO Tour Llif3" while X was still alive, it did become a No. 1 hit following his murder.

In the months, and now years, leading up to and following his death, X has morphed into a mythical creature, less of a deeply troubled symptom of larger systemic failings in America and more a means of litigating ethical consumption in music. Or, as a window into the violent fantasies embedded into disadvantaged—and privileged, if we're being honest—young men. His music and public persona fulfilled a fantasy for young men in America. Yes, he's there for them with his evocative ballads, but he also taps into the inherent violence of being nurtured by the darkest elements of the streets. His music worked both because of its quality and because the more aggressive and disturbing elements of the material scratched a deeply rooted itch in his fans. Yes, the work is compelling. Its quality merits thinking so critically about X's role in reflecting social values through music.

Still, there is another part of me, as I write this, that sees him as a tragic, disposable figure to a series of bad actors using him to advance their own agendas, either monetarily or morally. The emptying of the vault of X's recorded music, and the dumping of said music into half-baked posthumous releases, even as I believe in the value of the archive for all artists, feels nothing short of nefarious. In the years since his death, X has become a pawn to prove a point about violence and being a moral arbiter vis-a-vis art consumption, without really exploring the meat of why these cycles and circumstances came to pass in his life.

In short, X is an easy example to pull out of a hat, but he was also a victim of brutality for most of his too-short life. He perpetuated that cycle of violence, without question, all while continuing to mean the world to millions of kids. They feel a sense of duty to protect his legacy, no matter how rabid and certifiably dangerous their actions online and in person. The beauty of X's music runs completely contra to the wickedness of his violence, but this doesn't bother a hurt kid. I have to imagine that as more time passes, as our society develops a richer vocabulary to discuss abuse, and as his fans grow older and more distanced from his tragic death, there will be a holistic critical reappraisal of XXXTentacion.

Emo Rap Goes Pop

It's not a matter of "when" emo rap goes pop, but rather, how it does so. Following the boom of "XO Tour Llif3," most charting emo rap had a bit of an overcorrection. With the majors firmly involved, the hits had to be less suicidal. The transition from "XO Tour Llif3" to the placid 2020 number one hit "Mood" by 24kGoldn and iann dior revealed a more docile, toyish side of emo. Many of the breakout hits following "XO Tour Llif3," those produced in the wake of the meteoric rise of Juice WRLD and XXXTentacion, were largely dulled in comparison to their predecessors. The edge of emo rap was sanded down into something you could bop your head to at a coffee shop. While certain practitioners of the form endured—BONES is still releasing like a madman; Dro Kenji, DC The Don, and others are raging emo rap perfectionists—the big-time hits transitioned into something less and less distinguishable from serviceable pop music.

Maybe it's not all the labels' fault. Following "XO Tour Llif3," emo rap became a genre so ravaged by loss, it became a question of whether this music would continue to be made following the tragic deaths of Lil Peep, XXXTentacion, and Juice WRLD. In some ways, it's easy to point at that streak of suffering and understand why the new class of emo rap hits sounds nothing like the originals. And yet, these songs still borrow heavily from their frameworks. Iann dior's 2019 breakout single "emotions" takes quite a few visual and written notes from Juice WRLD's star-making hit, "All Girls Are the Same." They even share a producer. The single appears on dior's debut mixtape, *nothings ever good enough*. The titling here, and across the project ("crash my whip," "who cares," "don't want to fall") have all the hallmarks of emo rap. Still, these songs lack the urgency of their predecessors. They feel stripped of the charisma of Juice WRLD, or the hyper-specific writing of Lil Peep, or the cutting adrenaline of XXXTentacion. They *work*, but not much else.

The game is given away from the title of iann dior's late 2019 debut album, *Industry Plant*. Litigating whether dior himself is a plant—that is, an artist with major-label backing who is manufactured to appear DIY and rake in fans while getting the major boost—is not interesting. The commodification of emo rap, which is what the album title implies, is far more compelling. *Industry Plant* tells a tale of selling out and fitting in, released on the same label that snatched up Trippie Redd following his breakout success. Dior's album doesn't necessarily have anything to do with the forefathers of emo rap, with gross Atmosphere joints or gothic underground hits from TeamSESH. With a flattened world, thanks to the digital streaming age, the new emo rappers' sights are set on the charts, and by popping off online, they'll hit them.

The streaming model is just one of the faculties at work popifying emo rap. The streaming economy and the latent trauma of the COVID-19 pandemic work in tandem to increase a particular type of loneliness. While it may fuel creativity—Kid Cudi's breakout hit "Day 'N' Nite" was all about isolation, and it stuck the landing—COVID continues to shrink opportunities for artists to cut their teeth in the same way the emo rappers of yore once did on touring circuits. Moreover, the pandemic reshaped the ways in which kids socialized and spent their time, largely exacerbating the isolation of being a teenager. Online communities were forged and forced to replace the more tangible communities kids had access to, and consequently, the music was made for the internet—not the stage, or the basement, or any other performance arena. As with the SoundCloud era, young artists were just an upload away from changing their lives. Careers could be launched without the artist ever reaching out and touching a fan as a performer, for better or worse.

As emo rap trends closer and closer to being a dressing for the pop canon, I look to the involvement of Travis Barker as a signal that even the lightest of emo rap signatures have broad appeal. Coupled with his prior history within hip-hop, blink-182's drummer began popping up on a bevy of emo rap songs, and even worked on a complete album (*NEON SHARK*) with Trippie Redd.[1] "We had a lot of the same things in common, as far as influences, from what he was inspired by like Nirvana or Deftones, blink or Green Day," Barker had said about Trippie. "He had influences within the genre which I guess I'm best known for. And, I had seen Trippie before, I had witnessed him basically cut all the music and singing acapella for an entire set, so I knew I was going to be able to make something awesome with him in a different genre because he could sing, he had great melody, great pitch, he was a star."[2]

Barker, one of the defining musicians of the commercial pop-punk movement and its subsequent nostalgia-fueled 2020s revival, finding a common thread with one of the faces of emo rap, Trippie Redd, is significant. Barker was also a fan of the late Lil Peep, whose insistence on guitar-heavy productions and tender whine—and reciprocal love for blink-182—made him an easy bridge between emo rap and the pop-punk outgrowth that followed it. His investment in emo rap acts can be seen as an attempt to legitimize the genre outside of its own orbit. It appears as though there is an idealized value to having his voice attached to a record, despite my confidence that Travis Barker is not single-handedly bringing emo rap back to his rock peers.

More interestingly still is the question of who among the remaining emo rappers is *allowed* to perform a pop exercise. The popification of the genre is as much a function of economics as it is a look into the racial dynamics shaping which emotions are coded acceptable for what people. It's the age-old question of genre as a segregationist practice. The wonder of, "Is this pop because of the mode of the music, or because of the appearance of the artist?" Within emo rap, the sweeping pop attempts, the connections with Travis Barker, are linked to a class of artist deemed more palatable by the powers that be. Whoever is easiest to sell to the American audience, that is who we can count on to be nudged or shoved into taking emo rap to pop radio. Proximity to whiteness and class status are just as much at play as the tones of the music being made.

Of course, this line of thinking arrives at the Machine Gun Kelly dilemma. The Ohio rapper-turned-pop-punk-revivalist has caught a frenzy of fans and drawn disdain as he shifted from his breakneck "Wild Boy" days in the early 2010s, to feuding with Eminem across a series of diss tracks, to ultimately employing the same guitar fetishization Lil Wayne did with Kelly's *Tickets to My Downfall* and *Mainstream Sellout* albums, released in 2020 and 2022 respectively.

With Travis Barker as his go-to producer, with a history of living through the height of blink-182 and performing pop punk and emo touchpoint covers, the question of Kelly's sincerity is second to what his pivot and the audience's reception of it represents. These records are hugely popular. Kelly himself, born Colson Baker, seems unfazed by the consistent critical takedowns of his work, touting Platinum plaques instead of licking any sore wounds.[3] *Tickets to My Downfall* debuted at No. 1 on the Billboard 200. Immediately, critics and skeptics began asking what it means for a white practitioner of hip-hop to so easily transition into rock music. "[Rock] needed a defibrillator," Machine Gun Kelly told *Billboard* in his 2022 cover story.[4]

Whether Machine Gun Kelly revived rock or inspired a revival of mallcore-era music has little to do with the value of his shifting *presence*. Colson Baker is a perfect example of the fluidity of genre, the acceptance of rapt personal experimentation, as long as the final product will sell to a majority white audience. Baker's makeover into a pink-guitar-touting rock star is less about music and more about the way whiteness expands genre definitions and limits them at once. Clearly inspired by the visual language of the late Lil Peep and the screeds of Juice WRLD, when Baker declares himself an artist by switching genre descriptors, it draws a collective sigh. The music, much like iann dior's, is fine. It's clear Baker cares. It's clear he's having fun with this new character. "Baker has had an uphill battle for credibility," Meaghan Garvey wrote for *Billboard*.

When Baker's team nods to his sincerity, I like to take a step back and remember as a listener and writer that I will never have access to Baker's interior life. His love of rock music, his emotional outpouring on social media and in interviews, appears genuine. Who are we to say otherwise? And yet, when he declares, "The 2010s was great for singers and rappers, and I was part of that. But I think we needed something else: we needed an instrument," such intense revisionist history feels cataclysmic to the preservation of emo rap and music altogether.

Maybe it isn't all bad. Perhaps the popification of emo rap will allow the genre to expand beyond its wildest dreams, and a nostalgia for the meatier material will come around to the mainstream. "XO Tour Llif3," the Machine Gun Kelly remix, wouldn't be the worst thing.

Don't Forget About $uicideBoy$

$uicideboy$ ARE A UNIQUE CASE. THEY ARE INFLUENTIAL AND foundational to understanding more immediately accessible emo rap icons like Lil Peep and XXXTentacion. They hew closer to the raging SoundCloud rap spurred on by artists in Southern Florida, and, though they hate this term, horrorcore, than the melodic whirl that had slowly taken over emo rap by the group's inception in 2014. They pack out shows. Their release schedule is frenzied. Their name strikes a chord with conservative critics. By all accounts, $uicideboy$ should be the most recognizable names in their genre. They clawed their way out of the underground and, with bloodied knuckles and broken fingers, found themselves leading one of the largest enterprises in the emo rap sphere, with few critical looks and even less so in the way of contemporaries singing their praises.

Cousins from Louisiana, rappers Ruby da Cherry and $crim follow in the lineage of BONES and Xavier Wulf, with their deep and disorienting discography and gruesome lyrical content. Their music is a direct descendant of '90s Memphis hip-hop culture. Ruby and $crim came together after a long and arduous stint of Cherry attempting to break out in the underground punk rock scene as a drummer and $crim looking for a way out of dealing drugs to get by. "It was pretty much like cutting the hand, bleeding, and making a pact that there's no plan

B, that if this doesn't happen by the time we're thirty, I'm blowing my head off," $crim told *Mass Appeal*.[1]

The duo's moms were sisters, raising them each on Cash Money records. Ruby da Cherry explained in an early interview with *XXL*, "As I got older I wasn't allowed to listen to rap anymore because apparently it influenced me in a bad way and then I got into punk rock.... Then I got subwoofers in my car and I was like it's back to rap. I was listening to some Curren$y, some Souls of Mischief, some Pharcyde, OutKast is my favorite group ever. I took it back and tried to dig deep for old New York shit, old West Coast shit. [$crim] shed the light on me as far as new school rap goes."[2]

For Ruby da Cherry, playing music was fundamental to his childhood. As early as seven years old, he was playing violin, dabbling with drums, and eventually picking up skills with lead guitar, piano, and bass. $crim, by contrast, got into DJing and production in his early teens, mixing in selling pills with producing for other artists and releasing beat tapes by nineteen. In 2013, the cousins each reached breaking points. It felt as though nothing was working for either one of them— and there was a dire sense life was seconds from being upended for them both. It was at this point that the cousins came together to form the most successful emo rap group since the genre's inception in the early 2000s.

The scope of their desperate beginnings develops a compelling narrative for the duo as the underground, independent rap heroes they eventually grew into, selling out large shows constantly, and helming their own festivals, to the bewilderment of critics.[3] That is, the boys are easy to root for and identify with. Their original story boils down to a sense of, "Fuck! Nothing is working, we have to keep *trying*," which feels uniquely American in its insistence on bashing your head into a wall until either your head cracks or the wall breaks down. There is an overstated intensity to the $uicideboy$ narrative, and the way each member presents themselves in press and to fans.

Constructing a neat history of $uicideBoy$' discography is a fraught experiment. The duo's online presence is packed to the brim with fan theories and alter egos to complicate the flurry of EP, mixtape, and album releases. Of note, they have an early feature from BONES, a breakout moment in 2015 that caught some press attention, and an early co-sign from underground Florida rap pioneer Pouya. Otherwise, $uicideBoy$ largely achieved success in a vacuum. The quick pace of $uicideBoy$' growth as hip-hop artists feels like a rebate for all the time the duo spent breaking their brows in other, lesser endeavors.

Their music is fiery and raw. They flay themselves open and scoop out their guts and organs to be used as decoration. The biggest song of their career, "...And to Those I Love, Thanks for Sticking Around," is a shouty emotional fight song clearly pulling from the Southern rap tradition. It is a series of convincing and well-constructed wails, crescendoing into "I'll be dead by dawn." The vocals here are nearly too sweet to be so bone-rattling, so intent on seeping into and overtaking the listener's bloodstream.

In that breadth, their best album to date, 2022's *Sing Me a Lullaby, My Sweet Temptation*, features the lightest touches of the duo's discography. This gives way to a greater emphasis on the pained melodies honed in the latter half of their career. Two years earlier, on "What the Fuck Is Happening," which lands on the same album as "...And to Those I Love," Ruby appears just as bewildered by his and his cousin's success as every critic. The difference, of course, being that Ruby da Cherry and the conceit of the song rests on a joke. Of course they're globetrotting overachievers. There was no other outcome for $uicideboy$ when they joined forces a decade ago.

Currently, $uicideboy$ have over eleven million sustained monthly listeners on Spotify and a handful of Gold and even Platinum RIAA-certified plaques. It jars the mind how a group who made a blood pact to achieve something in rap together, a group whose entire image is based on suicidal ideation and the perils of addiction, is lapping nearly every other artist and group in their class. Still, their influence on the emo rap scene ("Peep was a huge fan of us. He was hitting us up when we had like 3,000 followers on SoundCloud offering to pay us $100 for a feature"; "We brought [XXXTentaction] on his first tour, the South-side Suicide Tour,") is largely discounted or overlooked by critics.[4] Naturally, after a decade of grinding in the punk circuit to no avail, this incenses Ruby da Cherry, who shared the sentiments with *Complex* in 2018: "I feel like we're ignored a lot. We don't get a lot of credit that's due and I think it's bullshit."

Prospecting on the supposed ignorance of critics to the $uicide-boy$ franchise obfuscates the larger point Cherry and $crim make with their fastidious presence in hip-hop: emo rap, like emo rock, thrives off being ignored and maligned by the establishment. No doubt, a significant part of the $uicideboy$' appeal comes from how off-putting they are both in presentation and to the key cultural players in the hip-hop space.

Getting middling reviews on *Pitchfork* is a badge of honor for fans, who take the anger Cherry expressed back in 2018 and use it to mount a defense for their favorite group. In short, it is easier to treasure something that is misunderstood by an institution than it is to like the thing everyone else likes. To be a $uicideboy$ fan is to find yourself in a sea of equally tasteful weirdos, people who suffer and succeed alongside you, who *get it*, just like you. And though there are at least ten million folks who understand the duo at any given moment, they present themselves as a basement band running through the DIY circuit and crushing shows at the bottom of the bill.

While credit from critics feels like a losing game, the $uicideBoy$ fanbase is oak-strong, spurred on by the brutalist honesty Ruby and $crim apply to their music and live shows. "I saw the $uicideBoy$ tour last year [in 2021]. Thinking about that in terms of Atmosphere shows in 2003, it makes me think about going to see Promise Ring versus Fall Out Boy," author and *Stereogum* editor Tom Breihan recalls. "It got so much bigger and they're doing different things. $uicideBoy$ are more about 'We're all going through this,' and it's less jokey—but still kind of jokey. The dynamics are kind of similar. This was a relatively underground thing that got super popular."

$uicideboy$' curious popularity suggests they are on the cusp of mainstream success. Yet, their essence remains underground. Everything down to their tour flyers appears intentionally grimy, as though they are salt-of-the-earth artists who got a little mud on their good karma. Their music has no air of the radio hits you'd expect from a duo running an empire of this magnitude. That is, $uicideBoy$ moves bodies with their music, and they have achieved something monumental for artists who blew up online, getting scores of people into seats for shows.

Their numbers speak to the dissonance between critical reception and fan loyalty. It is easy to write off Ruby and $crim—two white rappers who could easily be labeled as appropriating Southern rap for financial gain—but a more charitable approach to their artist personas reveals there is no persona at all. $uicideBoy$ began with an all-or-nothing promise of seeing dreams through to the bitter end, and there is little in the music that suggests this promise has been broken.

"$uicideboy$ aren't showmen in a traditional sense," Breihan wrote of the 2021 concert he attended. "They dress bummy. They don't wear jewelry. They look like guys who have been through some things, which is what they are. But they can own a room.... And they have a real empathetic connection with their audience, the kind of thing that can't be faked. $crim told the crowd, 'We may be up here, but we struggle. We all got our mental health problems. We got our addiction problems. We got problems in general.' I believe them. Maybe $uicideboy$ are hitting new levels right now because everybody has fucking problems, because some of us aren't even trying to pretend otherwise. Maybe the world needs a rap group that's ready to wallow in it with us."

On paper, then, $uicideBoy$ make perfect sense in the history of emo rap. They take the DIY ethos of early Atmosphere records, blend it with the necessary elements of Southern rap history—though they've been slammed with lawsuits for sampling Three 6 Mafia[5]—and avoid any potential grandstanding in the face of their incredible success. They're with *you*, and on stage, they make *you* feel like the only person in a sea of hundreds. They preach reciprocity and sobriety.[6] Their music is a tour of the gallows—but is also a vehicle to heal. In much the same way XXXTentacion spoke directly to his fans to establish a sense of family, Ruby and $crim use their music and live show to extend a hand out to anyone who is struggling, including each other. In 2020, the pair recommitted to sobriety and therapy.

"I was a junkie five years ago, and if it weren't for this kid right here, I'd be dead. But he pulled me out of that rut," $crim said two years prior to their recommitment, referencing Ruby da Cherry, in 2018. "And it all correlates to the whole dying-before-thirty thing because we literally made a blood pact and were like, 'We're gonna make this happen by any means necessary. We're not giving up on one another.' We stuck to it and that was the hardest I ever worked in my life."

Juice WRLD and the Question of the Archive

Jarad "Juice WRLD" Higgins: [Life before music] was boring. I mean I was still making music, but I was staying with my mom, figuring out what the fuck I'm finna do. I wasn't going to college, I couldn't work a job. I'm a very intelligent person and I always tested way above average than my grade, but I couldn't just sit there and do homework, or be in a classroom. Even with a high school diploma in Chicago, you can't really do that. You can get a factory job. But I couldn't just sit in the factory either. I worked in a car factory for like a month and I got fired. Maybe in less than a month. There was somebody next to me, like sixty years old doing the exact same job I'm doing, and he was going on like, "Well after you stay for this long and after you stay for that long you can get these benefits," like, "bro fuck off, this is fucking 8 Mile." Fuck all that bro.[1]

I was just doing what I knew and that was posting music. I have a very big library of shit that I like to listen to and that's how I communicate, through making music. It was natural, I never paid for promotion or bought followers. It's always been authentic and when I took a step back from everything and realized that's what it was, that's when I was like, "Okay, this is me." One day I realized that I'm not living anybody else's life but mine. I feel like people try to live other people's lives or worry about what other people think about their life. That's not the way to live at all. I realized that's it my life and that I'm the one painting the picture that's going to be left, so why not do everything my way?[2]

* * *

THE SOARING HEIGHTS OF HIP-HOP AND POP STARDOM AND THE downtrodden tropes of emo rap were melding together by the mid-2010s. Emo rap's modalities were absorbed into the broader rap consciousness, adopted into various strains of a new class of Southern and Midwestern pain music. Warbled verses and big, moody choruses were a staple of rap's younger generation. The traveling success of Lil Uzi Vert's "XO Tour Llif3" laid a foundation for emo rap to break out of its digital shell and touch listeners across the country. A young Chicago artist by the name of Juice WRLD was right on Uzi's heels, about to reshape the landscape of emo rap and hip-hop's reach in the mainstream by trilling about heartache while boasting an irresistible smile.

Juice WRLD began rapping seriously at sixteen years old, after years of playing piano, guitar, and other instruments. His time in music classes dated back to age six. He would join the school band in high school but eventually move on after discovering the ease at which he could record and upload his raps to SoundCloud. This origin story of a bedroom artist discovering SoundCloud is close enough to his contemporaries—Lil Peep especially—but there was the added wrinkle of Juice coming out of Chicago and sounding unlike anything the city was producing at the time. With his steady diet of Chief Keef and Lil Durk records to guide him between his two pillars of blunt raps and enchanting melodies, Juice would quickly go from underground talent to generational superstar.

By eighteen, Juice WRLD was on the verge of breaking nationally and doing feature interviews with rap publications. His rapid and explosive rise represented the speed at which stars could be made with the tech available to scrappy and determined kids. But before Juice WRLD was the chart-topping, Diamond hit-making artist who helped reshape hip-hop through his sincerity, he was going by Juice The Kidd, throwing his music up on SoundCloud in hope of something landing, and dropping a series of EPs that telegraphed the artist he would grow into.

Released in January 2016, *JUICED UP* was Higgins's debut. The sing-rapping on "I SWEAR" that opens the project lacks the charisma and confidence of Juice WRLD's breakout moments, but it does have the lyrical content that would come to define his biggest hits. "I SWEAR" was a budding heartbreak anthem, hinging on replacing women with other women alongside a bevy of boasts undercut by emotional pain. "RUNAWAY FREESTYLE," a freestyled remix of Kanye West's "Runaway," saw Juice tackling a disconcerting emotionality and drug abuse and featured him mumbling, "I'm struggling, struggling, struggling," with a humble tone two-thirds of the way through the song. "RUNAWAY FREESTYLE" was soft and lurching, while "Pretty Boy" revealed the Chief Keef influence. This song was closer in style to the South Florida rap scene Juice was likely encountering online—the XXXTentacion-fronted wave that would take over SoundCloud and also feature close-but-not-quite emo rappers like Smokepurpp, Ski Mask The Slump God, and more.

"Pretty Boy" was a curious case. The song differed dramatically from the music Juice would be known for nationally. It was aggressive, almost grating. Still, it would play just as important a role in understanding his legacy, especially as Juice went on to release tracks like "Syphilis" and "Big," team up with Ski on "Nuketown," and do consistent, brutish, hour-long freestyles to wow listeners. "Pretty Boy" revealed an element of Juice WRLD's growing into his voice and added texture to his origin story as a Chicago rapper with a sensitive heart.

"From my conversations with other people about Juice, it doesn't seem like his learning to rap was as social," music critic Paul Thompson recalls. "His learning seemed, to me, to be much more in his bedroom. One of the interesting contradictions of his, is usually you can hear someone's music and guess where they learned to rap. I do think the emotionality and how his music is about his interior life, definitely reveals the bedroom side of things, except the thing that complicates that is he is such an incredible freestyler."

The archive of Juice WRLD radio freestyles spans hours upon hours of freewheeling bars. Higgins was a boundless creative with a strong passion for language and the manipulation of language. His freestyles were gutsy and felt worlds away from the wounded croons that launched him into immediate and expansive fame, but there was no chasm between his ability as a rapper and as a popstar. Juice WRLD had immense range. He took the rock star aesthetic of Lil Wayne *and* the workman-like means by which Wayne recorded and released—and fused them together to build a strong foundation for the Juice WRLD project.

Juice WRLD's first radio interview took place alongside rapper and mentor Lil Bibby. Juice signed to Bibby after hitting the radar of Chicago's DJ Victoriouz, and connecting with label Grade A's G-Money. "I look up to people like Billy Idol and Jimi Hendrix, old legends," Juice said before Bibby interjected with a jab about all the rock band shirts Juice wore.[3] For Juice WRLD, wearing his influences, literally, on his chest flows in the same vein as Atmosphere releasing *Seven's Travels*, a series of emo vignettes and *God Loves Ugly*–era recordings, on punk label Epitaph. These sweet moments of inspiration all speak to one another. When Leor Galil wrote "How Atmosphere accidentally predicted Juice Wrld" back in 2018 for the *Chicago Reader*, he was hitting on something greater than the substance of each artist's music. Even if the aesthetics did not match, there was a sense of respect for the indie and underground scenes.

Juice's music career moved quickly thanks to the wildfire of internet curation: "When 2018 started, everything just took off. That's the only way I can describe it—it's like a rollercoaster, and instead of it slowing down, it's just getting faster, and faster, and faster," he told *NME*.[4] Following his first radio interview, he connected with young music video director and digital tastemaker Cole Bennett. The pair became fast friends as they recorded the music video for "All Girls Are The Same."

At the time, Bennett's *Lyrical Lemonade* YouTube channel was growing into a hotbed for artist discovery. "Bibby sent me a ton of Juice's music," Bennett told *GQ*.[5] "And I was like, 'Yo, this is crazy!' I fell in love with it right when I heard it." The pair's first video was released on February 25th, 2018. It was an instant success and brought his music out from the annals of SoundCloud and to the plates of interested critics. "Juice WRLD establishes himself as a compelling new player in the SoundCloud rap universe," wrote Sheldon Pearce for *Pitchfork*, naming the tune the Best New Track in March 2018.[6] It has since become a multiple-Platinum single in the United States. To this day, fans flock to the video's comments to share memories and experiences listening to "All Girls Are The Same" and remembering Juice WRLD's generational artistry.

"The tone that Juice is writing in, there's nothing really playful about most of it," Thompson says of the single's success. "It's pretty pained, and naked, and desperate. There's not a lot of irony. Especially when you think of a lot of emo bands, say from California, if they had a song called 'All Girls Are The Same,' there would be like six layers of irony. With Juice, it just sounds like he's *hurt*. The barrier to entry is low—there's no subtext. The song titles, look at how literal and open all of it is. That's a lot of why it lands."

Every Juice quotable is a plain-stated but emotionally intense declaration. "Tell me, what's the secret to love? I don't get it," Juice sang overtop Nick Mira's production. In the video, Juice's demeanor was as pained as his writing, his head slumped, his eyes often shut tight, processing his anguish. There were no walls up; each line direct as possible, putting the emotion and the urgent need to exorcize it from his system ahead of everything else. "All Girls Are The Same" was an excavation mission. Unlike the material on *JUICED UP*, this song went deeper and felt stickier. There was broad sadness on *JUICED UP*, but here were Juice's needling and raw nerves. In the realm of emo rap to that point, alongside the work of Lil Peep and XXXTentacion, this music felt brand new to a generation of young people. It was very base.

"I don't think of mid- and late-2010s emo rap as being descended from early 2000s emo rap," Thompson remarks. "He would play with the textures of rap and rock from the 2000s, but the songs are these really elemental things: 'I'm never gonna know love like I knew, and I'm so heartbroken, and I can't trust her, but she's the only one I can trust.' These are things that go back to the beginning of songwriting."

In the case of Juice, and emo rap as a broader genre and subculture in the 2010s, there is little need to reach back to the genesis of songwriting. Juice WRLD and his contemporaries are eager and direct descendants of a critical emo institution: the rock festival. "The whole Warped Tour scene, everything, that's where I got my start," Internet Money producer and Juice WRLD collaborator Taz Taylor tells me. "That's where I became a fan of rock music. I remember growing up on Sum 41, Yellowcard! Juice listened to *a lot* of Yellowcard.... Juice would do the vocal melodies inspired by the pop-punk shit, but on different types of beats. Whenever people look at somebody coming out of Chicago...at the time you got Keef, Chance The Rapper, and drill, the fact that Juice is coming out with emo shit and Bibby's out here supporting it! All the rap artists you wouldn't expect to fuck with Juice, they listened! He was the one that made [emo rap] more acceptable. Everybody felt like they could get into it."

Juice WRLD was, whether he intended to or not, working tirelessly to break the molds in place for young Black men in the Chicago music scene. At the time, it felt as though critics were eager to tell a tale of two

Chicagos, to the end of painting the city and its inhabitants as inherently violent. They would pit the drill music from G Herbo against the softer and poppier tones of Chance The Rapper, the trauma-informed poetics against the high-school-class-clown image, to try and prove one avenue of art was superior to the other. Juice WRLD's music added another wrinkle to that binary. He made it all the more difficult to reduce Chicago rap into a narrative of infighting—and expanded the way these men were allowed to express themselves.

"There's no such thing as pitting me against Chance," G Herbo told me in 2018.[7] "We're brothers. [Chief Keef and I] are a completely other side of Chicago, and we do represent a different Chicago life, but we all come together as one. Me and Chance come together as one on many occasions so you can see that you can have motivation, you can have two kids from totally different sides of the city coming together for one cause. We're shining a bright light on Chicago; that's what we all do.... So there's not no 'other side' of Chicago. People from different lifestyles can come together for the same cause."

Juice WRLD was erupting in the national scene at the same time G Herbo was explaining how holistic Chicago music really is—it was a moment where, in a post–"XO Tour Llif3" universe, listeners and white critics were becoming more welcoming of Black men emoting. "If hip-hop has historically focused on invincibility, this generation is fixated on mortality," New Yorker staff writer Carrie Battan wrote a few months before Juice WRLD blew up. In "Lil Xan and the Year in Sad Rap," Battan recounted 2017's emo rap highs and drastic lows.[8] She massaged out the poppy anguish this generation was working towards. Once listeners caught on, Juice WRLD revealed he would be at the apex of this glossy pain.

"I was going through a lot of shit and I wanted to take the hell that I'm in and turn it upside down," Juice WRLD said in an early Elevator interview feature.[9] He was speaking about his biggest-to-date project, 999, a nine-track tape produced by frequent collaborator Nick Mira and

DT. "I wasn't even gonna make a tape," he said. "I just went to the studio for a long ass time, and I locked myself in there and made 80 percent of the tape."

From *JUICED UP* to 999, Juice WRLD had nailed his evocative sound. His voice was clearer than ever, and the melty quality of his production choices played an even bigger role in building that dense, purple atmosphere. "Juice had a very, very strong sense of his on-record style from 999 on," Thompson agrees. "He had a tonal anchor on all his stuff, and that allows him to expand the margins of what a Juice WRLD song is, without seeming like there's no such thing as a defined Juice WRLD song. He could have a bunch of different styles, but there was something unifying."

999's "rainbow" leaned into trappier percussion, with an extra emphasis on lowkey piano lines and glittering flourishes. Juice balanced his insistence on unleashing a storm of bars with his singing. "If you look at Juice WRLD, he has his original hit singles 'All Girls Are The Same' or 'Lucid Dreams,' and those fit into the genre. With Lil Peep, it's more rap parlance. He's speaking like a rapper, but not rapping like one. Juice WRLD did *both*," writer Matthew Strauss says. "Lost her" captures this duality best with Juice hitting high notes about his pain after rapping and ad-libbing cheekily about his "roster" of hoes.

Where "All Girls Are The Same" brought Juice WRLD into the national rap conversation, "Lucid Dreams," and the subsequent music video directed by Bennett, established him permanently just a few months later. The Sting-sampling, currently RIAA Diamond-certified song was first released in June of 2017 with the rest of 999 before getting a major label release in May of 2018. The song peaked at No. 2 on the Billboard Hot 100 in early October 2018. "Lucid Dreams" was and remains a generational record, but it was made in only twenty minutes once Juice WRLD got to the studio. "If I'm not mistaken, I wrote it in April, May [of 2017]. I was a senior in high school, and I was in my family room at home, sitting against the couch...I pieced it together like a puzzle," Juice told *Billboard*.[10] "It wasn't rushed. I remember it was storming pretty bad that day...I think the power almost went out or something, it was crazy."

"I don't know how you come to that level of proficiency on [freestyling] and then, 'Okay, I'm gonna make "Lucid Dreams.'" That seems like ten years of progression in style, in multiple directions, and he wasn't doing it in conversation with anyone," Thompson remarks. "It became pretty obvious, pretty quickly, that he was a generational talent. I don't want to overstate how Juice was a huge departure, but he was doing it differently than everyone in Chicago when he came out. And it's a perfect storm: he's attractive, young, can *rap*-rap. And part of it is, he could try out a bunch of different stuff stylistically and nothing was going to stick to him if it didn't work out. He was dropping so much music, and tapping into so many audiences, he was free to try anything."

For Juice WRLD, his prolific nature was both a shield and a mark of freedom. He was able to do a bounty of emotional bloodletting with relative ease, breaking out song after song in quick succession. His music bubbled up quickly—his vault was brimming with gold. From the song titles to the lyrics, there's very little in the way of coyness to obscure Juice as a performing artist. Each song on his commercially released records had a distinct nakedness that hooked listeners immediately. Young kids looking for cathartic release didn't have to pick apart Juice's meanings to get to the good part: feeling better. Instead, Juice created an awesome swell of emotion and together, as a community, everyone rode it to shore.

"The *999* mixtape...when you have this entirely different feeling of people just opening up over guitar beats, rapping about how they *feel*? These conversations don't get sparked a lot, and it allows you to get more comfortable with yourself," rapper midwxst shares. "Juice, it was all about being openly yourself and creating what you want. No boundaries exist. You can do what you want to do, as long as you put your heart to it. I go way back with listening to Juice. He was one of my favorite artists. You can resonate with somebody who's so themselves and who's not scared to have people see them, because they're comfortable with who they are."

Midwxst, who is his own brand of chameleonic sad rapper, building a name for himself during the COVID-19 pandemic wave of discordant intensely online underground artists, is but one of the many acts Juice WRLD influenced. Midwxst represents a new generation of young Black artists growing increasingly confident being very, very sad on records—speaking openly about suicide and mental health. His music is in direct conversation with Juice's, both stylistically and lyrically. Though Juice WRLD's time in music was tragically brief, the impact of his vulnerability developed a distinct lineage in the emo rap to follow.

"I think it's important to add a personal aspect to your music—that's what makes it authentic at the end of the day," Juice had said. "I feel like that's what a lot of people are missing, when they're trying to make it into music. Sometimes, if it sounds good and if it reaches people's ears, it's gonna be a hit. But I feel like you have a better chance of reaching people if you speak from a personal standpoint."

Juice admitted a majority of his music prior was freestyled on the spot, but the insistence of writing and feeling out "Lucid Dreams" contributed to it being so resonant. The song, like much of the great emo rap before it, lacked pomp. It was a single dripping in accessible pain. Shadows of an ex crawling up the bedroom walls, the scorn of giving away your heart for nothing, moving on from a breakup so impossibly shattering, these are tried and true themes that Juice WRLD melted down and refashioned into a new mode of expression—even if he didn't believe the song would be a hit.[11]

"Lucid Dreams" positioned Juice as an emotional alchemist, turning the dregs of anguish into something glowing. The drama of the song, the heartbreak and the drug abuse, was met by a riptide of angst and concern for Juice. The music was just raw enough to make the listener wonder if Juice WRLD was standing at the precipice. Yet, cheekier lines like "Who knew evil girls had the prettiest face?" and "You were made outta plastic, fake" cut through worry. They were the grounding element that helped make "Lucid Dreams" feel like a conversation with a freshly dumped friend.

"'Lucid Dreams' is something that's very, for better or worse, similar to the kind of emo I loved when I was younger," author Hanif Abdurraqib shares. "It's so rawly about pain and heartbreak. Now, I know as an adult writer, thinker, and feeler, if you get your heart broken, it's perhaps better to work through it before taking it to the page. When I was younger, it was, 'I'm sad *now*.' So there's the immediate urgency, no matter what comes out. 'Lucid Dreams' has that vibe of, 'I'm sad; I had to produce *something*.' I could say the purpose of the song is meant to illuminate, but I don't know if that's what I feel. That's the magic trick of emo anything: sometimes the performance of the emotion obscures whatever the reality is."

"I would concede there's something undeniable to what he was doing," Thompson adds. "There are a ton of people who were trying for a version of Juice WRLD, but there was something about *him* that clicked. Some of it is industry machinations, and some of it is he cracked the code on records." By 2019, Juice said he couldn't stand "Lucid Dreams," perhaps an indication of how far-reaching and overplayed the song had become in his personal circles. It's a good problem to have, recording and releasing something so ubiquitous, you'd rather hear a different tune.

Juice WRLD released his debut studio album, *Goodbye & Good Riddance*, under Grade A and Interscope on May 23, 2018. "It's just a piece of myself I put out for people to hear," Juice said in a radio interview shortly after its release.[12] "Back in high school, even before that, I was good at freestyling," he told Zane Lowe the day before the album dropped.[13] "Then I started rapping, and I recorded a few records that didn't have any substance. I thought, *Why not put my heart into what I'm making?*"

In its final form—several tracks were added to the streaming release after the initial drop—*Goodbye & Good Riddance* ran just under fifty minutes and played out as the defining project of Juice WRLD's career. Housing "All Girls Are The Same" and "Lucid Dreams," the album was also home to a fitting Lil Uzi Vert cosign in "Wasted," the smash "Armed And Dangerous," the previously released "Hurt Me," originally titled "Sticks and Stones," and the Platinum-certified "Used To." This album was not exactly a full picture of his capabilities but was an enticing snapshot of what a prolific and heartfelt performer can do with the right team and resources. Of all his commercially released material, this is the album that gives listeners a fundamental understanding of Juice as an artist.

Goodbye & Good Riddance was packed with sneaky glimmers of superb imagery. "I know that these percies finna hurt me / Sometimes, I feel like they doin' surgery," Juice sing-rapped on "Black & White." His jubilant tone and the light touch of the production belied how gruesome the writing was here—particularly the idea that his body was being torn up by drugs. Later, on "Used To," he demanded to be buried in his sorrow before detailing a car-crash-fueled-heartbreak. His writing had an arresting starkness across his career.

The album debuted at No. 15 on the Billboard chart, eventually peaking at No. 4. It has since gone triple-Platinum in the US, and Platinum in several other countries despite lukewarm reviews from *Pitchfork* and *HipHopDX*. The 6.4-scored *Pitchfork* review read: "*Goodbye & Good Riddance* is an adolescent breakup record, and it's accordingly cathartic, petty, and clumsy in its emotional processing. It's as hard to like Higgins as it is easy to pity him."[14] By contrast, *DX* assumes a moralistic approach, warning that Juice's constant drug references have consequences: "One can only hope that *Goodbye & Good Riddance* doesn't influence the youth to turn to copious amounts of drugs when faced with unrequited love."[15]

Both reviews speak on the "emotional immediacy" of Juice's writing, and though their scores are identical—DX gave this record a 3.2 out of a possible 5 stars—the *Pitchfork* review feels more forgiving and excited for Juice's future. So much of the emo rap canon was met with negative and, at times, jokey criticism, and Juice's work was no different. Music as raw and direct as Juice WRLD's doesn't automatically secure a critical pass because of the subject matter or the delivery. The closing argument of the *Pitchfork* review included a nod to this album as having "crystallized the sonic footprint of this emo-rap moment." For as impressive as Juice's rise was in regards to its swiftness, perhaps more exciting is the quickness with which he captured lightning in a bottle.

"My end goal is to leave one of the biggest impacts on the world," Juice WRLD told *Complex* a month before his debut release. "Music is the doorway and how I express myself, but overall I just want to make [a] really, really big impact on the world. In a good way."

"It speaks to a part of me that I don't always give a voice," said Juice fan Alani Richardson in an interview with *MTV*.[16] "Most of us are dealing with feelings that are deeper than what we're able to express to our friends and family. His music was able to tap into those heavier emotions that I hadn't been able to express without being judged." Another fan added: "There have been so many days where I've felt isolated and alone and come home to turn on *Goodbye & Good Riddance*."

Juice's debut album may have not landed with critics, but it did what it was meant to do: connect to fans worldwide. Less than a year after *Goodbye & Good Riddance*, Juice WRLD released his blockbuster sophomore album, *Death Race For Love*. It would be his last. Debuting at No. 1 on the Billboard 200 chart, it has since gone multi-Platinum. *NME* rated it favorably, praising Juice's range and reverence for hip-hop's past, while looking towards the genre's future.[17]

Death Race for Love showed Juice WRLD dealing in a nostalgia all his own, from the video-game aesthetics featured in the cover design and select music videos, to his ear for classic rap samples, and from the poppish tones that made him famous to the brute force of rap that captivated purists whenever he crossed their radar. The album is Juice in real time, a dynamic piece of art meant to be a conduit for assessing who Juice WRLD really was, and who he could become. Lead single "Robbery" and subsequent single "Hear Me Calling" leaned on the appeal of "Lucid Dreams," while tracks like "Big" and "The Bees Knees" present a more aggressive demeanor.

"We made 'Robbery' in either December 2017 or January 2018," Nick Mira shared with *Billboard*.[18] "It was just so different than the stuff he was making at the time. When I made that beat, I wasn't really doing any ballad type records. I was mainly doing ambient and spacey stuff. With the melody, he sang over it perfectly. He texted it to me the week he made it and I thought it was amazing. It's my favorite song he's made to a beat of mine."

"I [was] making ['Hear Me Calling'] in the studio on New Year's Eve," producer Purps told *Billboard*. "I was going for more of a pop vibe, switching up from our normal stuff. I wasn't going to play it for him, but it was in the batch of beats for him. Max Lord [Juice's engineer] pressed play on it and as soon as Juice heard it, he was like, 'Whoa, whoa, whoa. I really like this.' He knocked that out within the hour. It was super catchy."

Juice's speed would evidence itself in the form of the album, how it swings between moods and runs seventy-two minutes on the standard version with only a fuzzy finish line in sight. "I recorded [*Death Race For Love*] in four days," Juice told *Vulture* in early March 2019.[19] "I wasn't self-conscious about dropping music no more. I wasn't self-conscious about the album anymore. I don't like that whole competing with myself thing, trying to top myself. It's good to have goals and to keep climbing, you know, but the music is gonna speak for itself. So just me realizing all those things, it kinda calmed my nerves about the new album. I just know I poured my soul into it. Every song but two or three of them on the new album are all freestyles, all made up in those four days."

"If you think too much, you'll start drawing blanks. You'll start overthinking it," Juice said. This gut instinct set *Death Race* apart from *Goodbye & Good Riddance*. While his debut was a strong entry in the emo rap canon, one that continues to define the genre today, *Death Race* was an ode to Juice WRLD's seemingly endless creative potential. The young artist was reaching for every corner of his influences, bringing them into his world, and reshaping them in his image.

"It's cool to have themes," Juice told *Vulture*. "It's cool to have structure. But at the same time, you create your own structure. There's a difference between madness and coordinated madness. You don't have to follow the rules of any book, as long as you have your own rules and follow them. So I just kind of made up my own structure; it's tied together because of the way I did it."

"For me, it was 'Bandit,' the Youngboy collab," Paul Thompson says of the most effective Juice WRLD song. "Bandit" was added to *Death Race* as a bonus track—track 11—in an updated version on streaming services. "Youngboy has this style that codes differently as Southern street rap, but is tapping into the same sort of raw emotionality as Juice WRLD. To hear Juice's style slightly recontextualized in that way largely unlocked him for me. I don't like it more because Youngboy's on it; I like it because it's clarifying for me things that exist in Juice that don't depend specifically on nostalgia plays."

"Bandit," the languid and pained "Fast," the purist's dream that is "10 Feet," and the album's other massive swings represent the heart of a twenty-year-old, and their passion cannot be ignored, even if the lines don't always land, as on "HeMotions," which is perhaps *too* direct. At over an hour, it's nearly impossible to hit home run after home run, but when *Death Race* achieves points of lucidity, the album soars. "My soul's empty, so deep, ten feet," Juice raps with a subtle snarl. It's one of the few moments on *Death Race* where there's no obscuring devices, vocal or otherwise, between us and Higgins. Elsewhere on "10 Feet," Juice proved himself to be a poetic mastermind. But it's the way Juice's voice landed so bare on this song that transformed it into a looking glass.

By the release of *Death Race*, Juice WRLD was playing to massive crowds, and the archival footage revealed nothing short of a rock star. Blaring backing guitars, elastic momentum on stage, and Juice's slight tweaks to his lyrics while singing made for a compelling stage presence that was always one sweeping drop away from taking down the venue. Though he was young, it seemed by 2019 that Juice had cracked the code for his onstage persona, never letting the vocal track overtake his performance. His wails and shouts coupled with the way he worked the stage and engaged his fans made even his biggest festival performances feel communal.

When comparing the smaller emo rap shows to the heights Juice WRLD reached, the sweaty mosh pits of early Peep concert footage and the way Juice effortlessly commanded thousands of folks with his emotional overtures, makes Juice's impact appear seismic. These shows were about exchanges of energy and the intensity of the conversations listeners and artists engage in when the music is this raw. The growth between Juice's smaller stateside shows in 2018 to the worldwide success and massive stages he graced by 2019 was monumental—meteoric in a literal sense. Juice WRLD was tapping a seemingly overflowing vein of potential.

Good emo rap presents itself as a conduit of self-discovery for the listener. The reason fans latch onto and become one with music largely revolves around this idea that Juice WRLD et al. are speaking from a place these listeners cannot themselves yet access. By mapping their experiences onto Juice's music, there is community made in the *aha* moments when a fan is in their room alone, on a walk, driving somewhere. This was the magic of *Goodbye & Good Riddance*: these instances where you whip around and say, "Oh, me, too!"

But *Death Race* seemed less interested in being an immediate conduit. Songs like "Empty" and "Who Shot Cupid?" were closer to exceptions than rules. *Death Race* was a lawless album where Juice used his shield of productivity to explore *himself* more openly. The result was clumsier, but perhaps in some instances more sincere to the growth of the young artist outside of music. There were clear signs Juice was pursuing a newfound maturity in the small window between albums, and one of the greatest tragedies is facing the truth we will never know a Juice WRLD who can reflect and innovate to the fullest degree.

"I look back now, and a lot of the folks that were making the music I was loving at sixteen, seventeen, looking for emo records, a lot of those folks weren't much older than I was at the time," Abdurraqib says. "They didn't really have a relationship with the kind of maturity that would lead to the kind of introspection that is at the heart of these well-done emotional explorations. That's not letting anyone off the hook. It's just, there's a point at which we have to realize, some of these folks did not have the tools in their toolbox to do what they needed to do."

Juice WRLD died suddenly on December 8, 2019. He was twenty-one. Two days later, *Vulture*'s Craig Jenkins published "We're Losing Another Rap Generation Right Before Our Eyes."[20] In the piece, Jenkins cataloged the "jarring losses" of artists in Juice's orbit—Lil Peep, XXXTentacion—and the losses of hip-hop artists exterior to emo rap: Mac Miller, Nipsey Hussle, and more. Juice's death being an accidental overdose resulted in an outpouring of moral panic about emo rap's relationship to drug use.

Jenkins wrote: "The tragic death of 21-year-old Juice WRLD this weekend reopened terrible old conversations about the relationship between rap music and drugs, and a shift from narratives about young men and women peddling illegal substances to stories about partaking.... There's greater danger in pills and powder than puff, puff, pass, but it's the wrong way to approach the matter. The substances of choice may have changed, but the animus for using hasn't.... You can't talk about drugs in rap without discussing drugs in America at large. There's an opioid crisis, and coke, lean, and meth are around every corner. That isn't the fault of any rapper. This generation didn't invent pills, powder, or lean. They aren't the first to introduce them to hip-hop."

Jenkins's writing continues on to underscore the constant presence of drugs in hip-hop and emphasizes how the moral panic of what young artists rap about obfuscates the greater point: they *have* to rap about these things, because these are their experiences, because these are our systems. Juice WRLD's cause of death was not mapped from the start because of his lyrical content.

On July 10, 2020, the first posthumous Juice WRLD album, *Legends Never Die*, was released. "From the bottom of our hearts we want to thank each and every one of you for your undivided adoration and love for Juice," his family shared in a statement.[21] "You guys meant the entire world to Juice and by listening to his music, watching his videos and sharing your stories about him, you are keeping his memory alive forever. We plan to honor Juice's talents, his spirit, and the love he felt for his fans by sharing unreleased music and other projects that he was passionately in the process of developing."

Legends Never Die was presented as a posthumous album in every facet of promotion. Certain tracks—"The Man, The Myth, The Legend" and "Juice WRLD Speaks from Heaven"—featured other artists praising Juice, or Juice speaking directly to his fans in an implied angel-like scenario. There was clear effort on the part of the personnel and the estate to make the record feel like a heartfelt send-off, and some of Juice's best material ("Righteous"; "Wishing Well") lives on this album. While several reviews questioned the exploitative nature of posthumous releases as a whole, the consensus was that this music did not add anything new to the Juice WRLD canon.

"This is bigger than emo rap—what does it mean to be a great rapper?" Thompson wonders when asked if he engages with Juice WRLD's posthumous material. "There's people who are like, the work is the finished album. The album is *the* creative statement. Finding drafts is not a reflection of who the artist is, but there are other people who argue that not all great rappers can make great albums. So, a rapper's 'work' is you imagining their whole catalog as one long unit of creativity. I don't get the impression that most of what would be in Juice WRLD's vault is radically less finished than the stuff that came out commercially. I don't think the songs we're gonna hear are going to be radically short of his vision for them.

"I wonder if maybe we should all be more generous to the idea that, with these very prolific artists, it's simply better to get a fuller picture of the stuff they were doing. Significant writers' personal and private correspondences will be published after their death. Visual artists' sketches will be displayed. We have to have faith that audiences will be able to understand and receive posthumous work differently. There's definitely something insidious because some of these posthumous albums are presented like the significant living works—that's a problem, for sure. As long as there's transparency, I think if we treat rap as serious art, we should give rappers the same treatment as [serious artists]."

As more and more Juice WRLD sketches reveal themselves, either as bonus tracks for already-released works, new posthumous titles, posthumous guest features, the instinct of the fan is likely twofold: to protect, and to indulge. But Thompson hits on something crucial when he notes almost every other medium of high art mines the personal archive of the dead to make a rounder public archive. The ethics around presentation and selling aside, these glimpses into Juice WRLD's extensive vault have their place if only because they are the illuminating factor. There is a whole archival exercise to be had in appreciating, dating, and understanding these posthumous works as greater than the gut impulse to call them money grabs.

The harrowing grief caused by Juice's passing continues to feel like a death knell for emo rap. Sure, there are imitators and young artists who borrow from his repertoire, but there can only be one Juice WRLD—only one artist so dedicated to being open and resonant. He was not as preoccupied with the ugly side of heartbreak as he was fascinated with what can happen when you flay yourself on record. His range came from his willingness to pivot his sound, as well as a sincerely unmatched creativity. He knew how to add wrinkles, how to kink a song just so. He was the bleeding heart of emo rap, and without him, that heart has all but dried up.

Outro

WRITING A BOOK ABOUT EMO RAP'S HISTORY IS KIND OF LIKE unwrapping a Kinder surprise egg and finding the toy inside this chocolatey delight has been smashed to bits. It's plasticky and more or less dusted. By the end of the 2010s, three of emo rap's key artists—XXXTentacion, Lil Peep, and Juice WRLD—had died tragically at the hands of gun violence and accidental overdoses. Every time I sat down to hammer away at this work, I was met with tremendous sadness. Shortly after Juice WRLD passed in 2019, I came across a score of tweets suggesting emo rap died the day Juice did—this hung over me daily. And yet, this immense pain was outdone by the immense pleasure of cataloging a meaningful movement in music and American culture.

Emo rap is a young person's genre in all the best ways. It's the music you play when you're all alone; it's the music you need to flow out of speakers or headphones and assume the form of a trusted, sometimes secret, companion. And even at its most depraved and unscrupulous, I find myself understanding the value of a young man expressing his pain into a shitty mic for the internet to devour. It is not novel in a historic sense, but it is seismic in a localized sense.

So much of this music's success is a product of technology advancing and the demands of the music industry changing rapidly alongside those leaps forward. When Atmosphere was bashing their heads in on the touring circuit, they had no idea they would be the genesis point of a movement. Their intensity around touring translated into an intensity to record—Peep, Juice, X, et al. unleashed themselves in real time. They learned from Lil Wayne. They digested their pain and threw it back up with relative ease. With the advent of streaming and the democratization of the music distribution model thanks to SoundCloud, there was nothing stopping a sea of young men from performing bloodletting rituals in the form of digitized howls. Their music was gnarly, imperfect, and exciting as it presented new ways to be yourself in hip-hop.

The history of emo rap is imperfect, and in many ways, *CRYBABY* is an imperfect reconstruction and critical examination of a genre that is felt more than articulated. The score of voices who open this book, who all struggled with the question, "So, what's emo rap?" illustrate the clumsy alchemy of the genre. These are artists who felt as though they were imbued with a forbidden knowledge. And though with some distance from their works, those among them who are still alive can attest everyone's been dumped once before, there will always be a new generation who feels their angst is the first of its kind. At one point, I toyed with the idea of asking my interview subjects who emo rap "was for," except I quickly understood that emo rap is *for* everyone. There is no age limit on feeling shitty, and you can't fall out of love with haunting memories of youth.

As new artists take on emo rap—midwxst, DC The Don, Dro Kenji—I wonder how the music will iterate upon itself. The sound of the mid-to-late 2010s has been folded and kneaded into popular culture. So, did emo rap die when Juice did? It is not a question of whether it will emerge in the new decade, but how—as in, how will emo rap develop, because the kids are going to need it to do so. Sooner or later, they're going to evolve it themselves, with screams, shouts, and wails. They'll tweak the tech, they'll redefine the language for all of their emotional firsts. Because the truth is, there will always be a rising class of kids getting dumped at the worst time of their lives. There will always be a suburban malaise to rage against. There will always be an eager generation of crybabies.

Endnotes

Atmosphere Gives Emo Rap Its Name

1 Shawn Setaro, "Rhymesayers At 20: An Oral History," *Forbes*, Nov 30, 2015. https://www.forbes.com/sites/shawnsetaro/2015/11/30/rhymesayers-20-an-oral-history/?sh=7836de52cca1.

2 Andy Greenwald, *Nothing Feels Good*, St. Martin's Griffin, November 15, 2003.

3 Tom Breihan, "*God Loves Ugly* Turns 20," *Stereogum*, June 10, 2022. https://www.stereogum.com/2189509/atmosphere-god-loves-ugly-turns-20/reviews/the-anniversary/.

4 Leor Galil, "How Atmosphere accidentally predicted Juice Wrld," *The Chicago Reader*, September 11, 2018. https://chicagoreader.com/music/how-atmosphere-accidentally-predicted-juice-wrld/.

Kid Cudi's "Day 'N' Nite" Introduces Sensitivity to Emo Rap

1 "Kid Cudi," *Complex Magazine*, August 3, 2009. https://web.archive.org/web/20130427174922/http://www.complex.com/music/2009/07/kid-cudi/page/2.

2 Pranav Trewn, "*A Kid Named Cudi* Turns 10," *Stereogum*, July 17, 2018. https://www.stereogum.com/2005961/kid-cudi-a-kid-named-cudi-10th-anniversary/reviews/the-anniversary/.

3 Spencer Kornhaber, "Kid Cudi Sparks a Conversation on Depression, Race, and Rap," *The Atlantic*, October 5, 2016. https://www.theatlantic.com/entertainment/archive/2016/10/kid-cudi-depression-rehab-yougoodman-rap-mental-health/502973/.

BONES Adds a Gothic Texture to Emo

1 Gabe Allanoff, "Bones Gives a Rare Interview About Love, Identity, and Fatherhood," *Interview*, July 13, 2021. https://www.interviewmagazine.com/music/bones-gives-a-rare-interview-about-love-identity-and-fatherhood

2 John Ruskin, "Nardwuar vs. Bones," *NardwuarServiette*, May 30, 2019. Video, 23:02, https://www.youtube.com/watch?v=nhsvSKGnUcw.

3 Max Bell, "A Bones Halloween," *Passion of the Weiss*, October 31, 2013. https://www.passionweiss.com/2013/10/31/a-bones-halloween/.

4 Duncan Cooper, "Download LA-via-Michigan Rapper Bones' Massive Garbage Mixtape," *The FADER*, June 09, 2014. https://www.thefader.com/2014/06/09/download-rapper-bones-garbage-mixtape.

Lil Wayne's Influence on Emo Rap

1 Samuel Hine, "Emo-Rapper Lil Peep Says His Fearless Style Is What Fashion Needs Right Now," *GQ*, August 18, 2017. https://www.gq.com/story/lil-peep-says-his-fearless-style-is-what-fashion-needs.

2 Christina Lee, Regina N. Bradley, "Gangster, Griot, and GOAT: Unpacking Lil Wayne's Reign and Reckoning," *Bottom of the Map*, August 22, 2021. Podcast, 1:04:19, https://www.bottomofthemap.media/episodes.

3 Nick Barat, "Lil Wayne: Eats Tapes," *The FADER*, September 27, 2012. https://www.thefader.com/2012/09/27/lil-wayne-eats-tapes.

4 Nick Barat, "Rap's First Millennial Grows Up," *The FADER*, January 09, 2017. https://www.thefader.com/2017/01/09/lil-wayne-best-rapper-alive-rap-millennial-grows-up-essay.

5 Andre Gee, "Lil Wayne Is So Prolific He Hardly Remembers 'Tha Carter III,'" *Rolling Stone*, June 9, 2023. https://www.rollingstone.com/music/music-features/lil-wayne-interview-carter-anniversary-1234766396/.

6 Simon Vozick-Levinson, "Lil Wayne's 'Prom Queen': Make it go away!," *Entertainment Weekly*, August 4, 2020. https://ew.com/article/2009/01/28/prom-queen-wayn/.

7 Drew Millard, "Is Lil Peep's Music Brilliant or Stupid as Shit?" *VICE*, December 23, 2016. https://www.vice.com/en/article/nznmag/is-lil-peeps-music-brilliant-or-stupid-as-shit.

8 Alphonse Pierre, "Lil Yachty: Let's Start Here. Album Review," *Pitchfork*, February 1, 2023. https://pitchfork.com/reviews/albums/lil-yachty-lets-start-here/.

Xavier Wulf Brings Memphis History to Emo Rap

1 Nathaniel Louis-Capois, "It's Time to Pull the Sword: An Interview With Xavier Wulf," *Complex*, Feb 27, 2018. https://www.complex.com/pigeons-and-planes/2018/02/xavier-wulf-interview-check-it-out-premiere.

2 "Interview: Raider Klan | Rvidxr Klvn Part 1 – The Memphis Edition (Chris Travis, Ethelwulf, & Yung Raw)," *Hardwood Blacktop*, August 14, 2012. https://philafanalytics.wordpress.com/2012/08/14/interview-raider-klan-rvidxr-klvn-part-1-the-memphis-edition-chris-travis-ethelwulf-yung-raw/.

3 "IAR Interview: Ethelwulf," *It's A Rap*, July 12, 2012. http://teamitsarap.blogspot.com/2012/07/iar-interview-ethelwulf.html.

4 "Exclusive Interview with Ethelwulf aka XavierWulf His 1st ever in person)," *historyofthearchivest*, April 29, 2013. Video, 14:22, https://www.youtube.com/watch?v=RF-3ygN2Lig.

5 "Xavier Wulf on Raider Klan, Seshollowaterboyz, Lil Peep, Skepta & More!," *Our Generation Music*, August 7, 2021. Video, 1:04:42, https://www.youtube.com/watch?v=5OBFxvnoF54.

6 "X. Wulf talks name change, preference in women, twitter & much more," *SAY CHEESE!*, January 22, 2014. Video, 13:49, https://www.youtube.com/watch?v=QsJ6vbGCnMo.

7 "Open Space: Xavier Wulf | Mass Appeal," *Mass Appeal*, May 9, 2017. Video, 10:28, https://www.youtube.com/watch?v=VPFfmRkSWTA.

8 "ETHEL WULF - LIVE IN SF," *Transylvanian Recordings*, April 17, 2013. Video, 8:12, https://www.youtube.com/watch?v=gYsQgSohfbI.

9 "SESHOLLOWATERBOYZ x MONTREALITY - Interview," *MONTREALITY*, June 5, 2019. Video, 14:30, https://www.youtube.com/watch?v=hDNMo2S1ojs.

Yung Lean Expanded the Definition of Emo Rap

1 Alex Gardner, "24 Rising Artists to Watch in 2024," *Complex*, January 24, 2024. https://www.complex.com/pigeons-and-planes/2016/04/yung-lean-2016-interview.

2 Jon Caramanica, "Yung Lean Evolves Into a Full-Fledged Practitioner," *The New York Times*, July 10, 2014. https://www.nytimes.com/2014/07/11/arts/music/yung-lean-in-new-york-a-rapper-evolves.html.

3 Jonah Bromwich, "Yung Lean: Unknown Memory Album Review," *Pitchfork*, September 24, 2014. https://pitchfork.com/reviews/albums/19827-yung-lean-unknown-memory/.

4 Max Bell, "Interview: Yung Gud," *Red Bull Music Academy Daily*, June 5, 2014. https://daily.redbullmusicacademy.com/2014/06/yung-gud-interview.

5 Emilie Friedlander, "'Taking Arizona Iced Tea and Making It Cry': An Interview with Yung Lean and the Sad Boys," *The FADER*, July 16, 2014. thefader.com/2014/07/16/taking-arizona-iced-tea-and-making-it-cry-an-interview-with-yung-lean-and-the-sad-boys.

6 Drew Millard, "Gud Wants to Make Music More Real And Less Internet," VICE, August 2, 2016. https://www.vice.com/en/article/53akbb/gud-spotlight-sad-boys-interview.

7 Thomas Hobbs, "'It Was All About Being Fearless:'" Clams Casino on 10 years of A$AP Rocky's 'LIVE.LOVE.A$AP'" *Okayplayer*, October 29, 2021. https://www.okayplayer.com/music/asap-rocky-live-love-asap-clams-casino-interview.html.

8 Duncan Cooper, "Yung Lean's Second Chance," *The FADER*, June 16, 2016. https://www.thefader.com/2016/06/16/yung-lean-warlord-interview.

9 Steffanee Wang, "Songs We Love: Yung Lean, 'Agony,'" NPR, November 15, 2017. https://www.npr.org/2017/11/15/564116363/songs-we-love-yung-lean-agony.

10 Rachel Aroesti, "'I'm genuine – and a bit strange': emo rapper Yung Lean bares his soul," *The Guardian*, May 12, 2020. https://www.theguardian.com/music/2020/may/12/im-genuine-and-a-bit-strange-emo-rapper-yung-lean-bares-his-soul-jonatan-leandoer-hastad.

11 Nico Walker, "Yung Lean: Doctor Said He's Gonna Be A Sad Boy," *Office*, October 2, 2022. http://officemagazine.net/yung-lean-doctor-said-hes-gonna-be-sad-boy.

Chasing the Light of 6 Dogs's Legacy

1 "6 Dogs is 17, Blowing Up On Soundcloud, and Grounded By His Mom," The Masked Gorilla. http://www.themaskedgorilla.com/6-dogs-rapper-flossing-interview/.

2 "6 DOGS EXPOSED," *No Jumper*, January 23, 2018. Video, 22:51, https://www.youtube.com/watch?v=L5JjcXp4oHU.

3 "6 Dogs (Full Interview) | HAM Radio," *All Def Music*, June 3, 2018. Video, 33:06, https://www.youtube.com/watch?v=1s_3Qq2sZIY.

4 "6 Dogs Interview - Masked Gorilla Podcast," *Masked Gorilla*, May 1, 2020. Video, 51:40, https://www.youtube.com/watch?v=Etox-Su12HQ.

5 Graham Corrigan, "When Stars Align: A Final Conversation with 6 Dogs," *Complex*, March 9, 2021. https://www.complex.com/pigeons-and-planes/6-dogs-ronald-interview-2021.

6 "6Dogs Sits Down With The Nuance Magazine," *NUANCE*, September 17, 2020. Video, 8:17, https://www.youtube.com/watch?v=9ZHTc-PnuHY.

7 Donna-Claire Chesman, "6 Dogs Producer Daniel Hartzog Breaks Down the Making of 'RONALD.,'" Audiomack, March 12, 2021. https://audiomack.com/world/post/6-dogs-daniel-hartzog-interview.

Where Are the Women?

1 Jessica Hopper, The First Collection of Criticism by a Living Female Rock Critic, Featherproof Books, May 12, 2015.

2 Marc Hogan, "XXXTentacion Confessed to Domestic Abuse and Other Violent Crimes in Newly Obtained Secret Recording," *Pitchfork*, October 23, 2018. https://pitchfork.com/news/xxxtentacion-confessed-to-domestic-abuse-secret-recording-listen/.

The Curious Case of Corbin

1 Hattie Collins, "Lose Yourself in the Sound of Corbin," *i-D*, February 9, 2015. https://archive.ph/S5py9#selection-2641.0-2641.36.

2 Chris Mench, Alex Gardner, Angel Diaz, Brandon Jenkins, Damien Scott, Dharmic X, Edwin Ortiz, Insanul Ahmed, Jacob Moore, Justin Charity, Justin Davis, Khal, Lauren Nostro, Ross Scarano, Zach Frydenlund, "The Best Songs of 2014 (So Far)," *Complex*, Jun 30, 2014. https://www.complex.com/music/2014/06/best-songs-of-2014-so-far.

3 Chris Riemenschneider, "Trying to decode MN's viral sensation Spooky Black," *Star Tribune*, October 2, 2014. startribune.com/trying-to-decode-mn-s-viral-sensation-spooky-black/277930421/.

4 Joe Price, "Corbin on the anger, isolation & paranoia of his debut album," *Dazed*, September 14, 2017. https://www.dazeddigital.com/music/article/37404/1/corbin-spooky-black-interview.

5 David Renshaw, "Listen To Corbin (F.K.A. Spooky Black)'s New Album Mourn," *The FADER*, September 5, 2017. https://www.thefader.com/2017/09/05/corbin-mourn-album-stream.

6 Pat Levy, "Corbin: Mourn Album Review," *Pitchfork*, September 19, 2017. https://pitchfork.com/reviews/albums/corbin-mourn/.

7 Donna-Claire Chesman, "Listen to Corbin's 'Tell Me': Re-Upped," Audiomack, November 2, 2021. https://audiomack.com/world/post/corbin-tell-me-re-upped.

Do We Love Makonnen?

1 Billboard Staff, "iLoveMakonnen Comes Out as Gay," *Billboard*, January 20, 2017. https://www.billboard.com/music/music-news/makonnen-comes-out-gay-7662435/.

2 "Real n****s go hard (pause, no homo): iLoveMakonnen," *Louder Than a Riot*, May 2023. Podcast, 55:12, https://open.spotify.com/episode/1lSZwNtCOQHm2JbKho9O2B.

3 Naomi Zeichner, "Meet ILoveMakonnen, The Eccentric Rapper Drake And Miley Cyrus Want To Be Down With," BuzzFeed, August 13, 2014. https://www.buzzfeed.com/naomizeichner/who-is-ilovemakonnen.

4 Sean Fennessy, "Hype Going Up (on a Tuesday): ILoveMakonnen and the Power of the Drake Career Boost," *Grantland*, August 27, 2014. https://grantland.com/hollywood-prospectus/ilovemakonnen-drake-club-going-up-remix-career-boost-makonnen/.

5 Lindsay Zoladz, "The 20 Best Songs of 2014," *Vulture*, December 12, 2014. https://www.vulture.com/2014/12/20-best-songs-of-2014.html.

6 Benjy Hansen-Bundy, "ILoveMakonnen on Becoming Famous Overnight," *GQ*, January 19, 2015. https://www.gq.com/story/ilovemakonnen.

7 "Makonnen addresses his sexuality and shades OG Maco!," *HOT 97*, December 9, 2014. Video, 31:50, https://www.youtube.com/watch?v=spdmtEF4gnM

Finding Lil Peep

1 Emma Garland, "A First Date in a Cemetery with Lil Peep," *VICE*, July 6, 2017. https://www.vice.com/en/article/a3dedg/first-date-lil-peep-interview.

2 Liza Womack, "Songs We Used to Sing, Listen to, and Read," *About Gus*, July 11, 2022. https://lilpeep.com/blogs/about-gus /songs-we-used-to-sing-listen-to-and-read.

3 Liza Womack, "Gus's Writing," *About Gus*, August 15, 2022. https://lilpeep.com/about-gus/archive/guss-writing.

4 Drew Millard, "Is Lil Peep's Music Brilliant or Stupid as Shit?" *VICE*, December 23, 2016. https://www.vice.com/en/article/nznmag/is-lil-peeps-music-brilliant-or-stupid-as-shit.

5 Colin Joyce, "Lil Peep Is the Artist of the Decade," *VICE*, November 6, 2019. https://www.vice.com/en/article/9kejgz/lil-peep-is-the-artist-of-the-decade.

6 Liza Womack, "Feelz," *Gus's Music*, May 20, 2022. https://lilpeep.com/blogs/posts-by-liza/feelz.

7 Jack Angell, "The Kryptik Interview," *Underground Underdogs*, March 8, 2018. https://undergroundunderdogs.com/2018/03/08/kryptik/.

8 "Lil Peep's Mom Liza Womack Talks About 'Cry Baby' 4 Years Later," *Masked Gorilla*, June 19, 2020. Video, 19:09, https://www.youtube.com/watch?v=WpWsBoulFqY.

9 "8 Lil Peep tracks that nod to some of the scene's most prominent artists," *Alternative Press Magazine*, July 14, 2021. https://www.altpress.com/lil-peep-samples/.

10 Donna-Claire Chesman, "'His Most Iconic Tape': Remembering Lil Peep's 'Hellboy,'" Audiomack, September 25, 2020. https://audiomack.com/world/post/lil-peep-hellboy-interviews.

11 Matthew Strauss, "Lil Peep: Hellboy Album Review," *Pitchfork*, November 18, 2018. https://pitchfork.com/reviews/albums/lil-peep-hellboy/.

Lil Uzi Vert's "XO Tour Llif3" Codified Misery in the Mainstream

1 Eric Skelton, "Playing With Fire: The Science Behind Lil Uzi Vert's Effortless Flow," *Complex*, August 31, 2017. https://www.complex.com/pigeons-and-planes/2017/08/lil-uzi-vert-hip-hop-flow-state.

2 "The Making Of Lil Uzi Vert's "XO TOUR Llif3" With TM88 | Deconstructed," *Genius*, June 9, 2017. Video, 6:34, https://www.youtube.com/watch?v=lH5ROxbKig4.

3 Billboard Staff, "Billboard's 100 Best Songs of 2017: Critics' Picks," *Billboard*, December 13, 2017. https://www.billboard.com/media/lists/100-best-songs-of-2017-critics-picks-8063600/.

4 Joe Coscarelli, "Have You Heard This Lil Uzi Vert Lyric?," *The New York Times*, August 13, 2017. https://www.nytimes.com/interactive/2017/08/13/arts/lil-uzi-vert-xo-tour-llif3-push-me-to-the-edge.html.

5 Carrie Battan, "Lil Xan and the Year in Sad Rap," *The New Yorker*, January 1, 2018. https://www.newyorker.com/magazine/2018/01/08/lil-xan-and-the-year-in-sad-rap.

6 Frank Guan, "Lil Uzi Vert Has a Modern-Day 'Smells Like Teen Spirit' on His Hands," *Vulture*, May 11, 2017. https://www.vulture.com/2017/05/lil-uzi-verts-own-smells-like-teen-spirit.html.

7 Sidney Madden, "Lil Uzi Vert Dance Sparks New Social Media Challenge," *XXL*, March 16, 2017. https://www.xxlmag.com/lil-uzi-vert-challenge-popularity-xo-tour-llif3/.

Raider Klan, SoundCloud, and GothBoiClique Gave Emo Rap Community

1 Alphonse Pierre, "How Denzel Curry Helped Pioneer SoundCloud Rap," *Pitchfork*, September 20, 2018. https://pitchfork.com/thepitch/how-denzel-curry-helped-pioneer-soundcloud-rap/.

2 Emma Garland, "Inside the Highly Strange World of Wicca Phase Springs Eternal," *VICE*, September 6, 2018. https://www.vice.com/en/article/ywkaby/inside-the-highly-strange-world-of-wicca-phase-springs-eternal.

3 "fish narc Is Ready to Sing Again," DJBooth, March 16, 2020. https://djbooth.net/features/2020-03-16-fish-narc-wildfire-interview-new-music.

4 Shakeil Greeley, "Lil Tracy Will Not Be Erased," *Pitchfork*, November 27, 2018. https://pitchfork.com/thepitch/lil-tracy-will-not-be-erased/.

5 Ezra Marcus, "Lil Tracy's Third Life," *The FADER*, March 7, 2019. https://www.the-fader.com/2019/03/07/lil-tracy-cover-story.

6 Adam Zamecnik, "'I Don't Want To Be A Rockstar' Cold Hart Interviewed," *Clash Music*, September 28, 2021. https://www.clashmusic.com/features/i-dont-want-to-be-a-rockstar-cold-hart-interviewed/.

7 Donna-Claire Chesman, "blackwinterwells Is Charting a New Music History," Audiomack, May 02, 2022. https://audiomack.com/world/post/blackwinterwells-interview.

Trippie Redd Gets Dubbed Emo Rap's Sinatra

1 Amal AlTauqi, "PAUSE Meets: Trippie Redd," *PAUSE*, January 19, 2022. https://pausemag.co.uk/2022/01/pause-meets-trippie-redd/.

2 Tyler Benz, "Trippie Redd Is on the Way to Becoming Soundcloud Rap's Frank Sinatra," *VICE*, August 11, 2017. https://www.vice.com/en/article/qvvp9v/trippie-redd-is-on-the-way-to-becoming-soundcloud-raps-frank-sinatra.

3 Max Weinstein, "The Break Presents: Trippie Redd," *XXL*, July 22, 2017. https://www.xxlmag.com/trippie-redd-interview-break/.

4 "Trippie Redd Interview (Uncut)," *Pigeons & Planes*, August 4, 2017. Video, 14:48, https://www.youtube.com/watch?v=UKDWVDGJbmo.

5 Waylon O'Day, "Trippie Redd Creates Emo Thrash Rap on 'A Love Letter To You,'" *Modern Life*, June 28, 2017. themodernlifemag.com/music/2017/6/28/trippie-redd-creates-emo-thrash-rap-on-a-love-letter-to-you

6 "Trippie Redd: A Lover Letter to You: User Reviews," Album of the Year. https://www.albumoftheyear.org/album/87239-trippie-redd-a-love-letter-to-you/user-reviews/.

7 Patrick Lyons, "Man On The Moon Turns 10," *Stereogum*, September 13, 2019. https://www.stereogum.com/2057868/man-on-the-moon-turns-10/reviews/the-anniversary/

8 "Honorable C.N.O.T.E. Never Heard Trippie Redd's Music Before Placing 'Dark Knight Dummo' Beat," *DJBooth*, December 21, 2017. https://djbooth.net/features/2017-12-21-honorable-cnote-dark-knight-dummo-interview.

9 Andy Hutchins, "Five Reasons Why XXL's Freshman Class Issue Is Going To Be A Yearly Ritual For A While," *The Village Voice*, February 28, 2012. https://www.villagevoice.com/2012/02/28/five-reasons-why-xxls-freshman-class-issue-is-going-to-be-a-yearly-ritual-for-a-while/.

10 "The XXL Freshman List & Hip-Hop's Industry of Delusion," *DJBooth*, June 13, 2016. https://djbooth.net/features/2016-06-13-xxl-freshman-delusion.

11 XXL Staff, "2018 XXL Freshman Class: We Got Clout," *XXL*, June 12, 2018. https://www.xxlmag.com/2018-xxl-freshman-cover/.

12 "Trippie Redd Is Rap's New Rock Star—2018 XXL Freshman Interview," *XXL*, June 28, 2018. Video, 2:03, https://www.youtube.com/watch?v=NXFSVoLGyIs.

13 Marisa Mendez, "The Unorthodox Life of Rap's Most Notorious Rock Star, Trippie Redd," *Bleu Magazine*, February 16, 2021. https://bleumag.com/2021/02/16/bleu-magazine-trippie-redd/.

What to Make of XXXTentacion?

1 Brian Josephs, "XXXTentacion's Alleged Domestic Abuse Detailed in Graphic Testimony," *Spin*, September 8, 2017. https://www.spin.com/2017/09/xxxtentacion-domestic-abuse-testimony/.

2 The State of Florida, "Miami-Dade Formal Charges," October 28, 2016. https://www.scribd.com/document/338234122/Miami-Dade-formal-charges.

3 Charles Holmes, "What's the Appeal of XXXTentacion's Music?," *Complex*, Aug 25, 2017. https://www.complex.com/music/2017/08/what-makes-xxxtentacions-music-appealing.

4 "The Xxxtentacion Interview," *No Jumper*, April 28, 2016. Podcast, 1:19:39. https://soundcloud.com/nojumper/xxxtentacionfinal.

5 Andre Gee, "On His New Single, Yvngxchris Pays Homage to XXXTentacion," *Rolling Stone*, January 23, 2023. https://www.rollingstone.com/music/music-features/yvngxchris-serenity-xxxtentacion-song-interview-1234666627/.

6 Joe Coscarelli, Julie Landry Laviolette, "XXXTentacion Is Mourned by Thousands at a Memorial in Florida," *The New York Times*, June 27, 2018. https://www.nytimes.com/2018/06/27/arts/music/xxxtentacion-funeral-died.html.

7 Jerrod MacFarlane, "The Rise of XXXTentacion and How the Internet Changed Hip-Hop," *New America*, October 9, 2020. https://www.newamerica.org/weekly/rise-xxxtentacion-and-how-internet-changed-hip-hop/.

8 Meaghan Garvey, "XXXTentacion: 17 Album Review," *Pitchfork*, August 31, 2017. https://pitchfork.com/reviews/albums/xxxtentacion-17/.

Emo Rap Goes Pop

1 Paul Thompson, "Give the Drummer Some Credit," *The Ringer*, July 27, 2022. https://www.theringer.com/rap/2022/7/27/23280164/travis-barker-emo-producer-punk-hip-hop-blink-182.

2 Sose Fuamoli, "Trippie Redd and Travis Barker on The Creation Of 'NEON SHARK,'" *Rolling Stone Australia*, February 23, 2021. https://au.rollingstone.com/music/music-features/trippie-redd-travis-barker-neon-shark-interview-23387/.

3 Tom Breihan, "Oh Boy, Machine Gun Kelly & Willow Smith Made A Song Called 'Emo Girl,'" *Stereogum*, February 4, 2022. https://www.stereogum.com/2175010/oh-boy-machine-gun-kelly-willow-smith-made-a-song-called-emo-girl/music/.

4 Meaghan Garvey, "At Home With Machine Gun Kelly, the New Prince of Pop-Punk," *Billboard*, March 23, 2022. https://www.billboard.com/music/features/machine-gun-kelly-billboard-cover-story-2022-interview-1235047603/.

Don't Forget About $uicideBoy$

1 Kate Robertson, "Who are $UICIDEBOY$ and how do they sell out shows around the world—including Auckland?," *The Spinoff*, May 9, 2017. https://thespinoff.co.nz/pop-culture/09-05-2017/who-are-uicideboy-and-how-do-they-sell-out-shows-around-the-world-including-auckland.

2 Emmanuel C. M., "The Break Presents: Suicideboys," *XXL*, April 7, 2017. https://www.xxlmag.com/suicideboys-interview-the-break/.

3 Tom Breihan, "The $uicideboy$ Circus Comes To Town," *Stereogum*, October 6, 2021. https://www.stereogum.com/2163161/suicideboys-live-show-grey-day-review/columns/status-aint-hood/.

4 Shawn Setaro, "Suicideboys Say They Influenced SoundCloud Rap—And They're Coming for Their Credit," *Complex*, Sep 12, 2018. https://www.complex.com/music/2018/09/suicideboys-say-they-influenced-soundcloud-rap-coming-for-their-credit.

5 Jordan Darville, "Report: Three 6 Mafia launch $6.45 million lawsuit against $uicideboy$ over samples," *The FADER*, September 08, 2020. https://www.thefader.com/2020/09/08/report-three-6-mafia-launch-s645-million-lawsuit-against-suicideboys-over-samples.

6 Kwase Lane, "$uicideboy$' sobriety is a renewal of spirit and promise," *Alternative Press*, August 1, 2022. https://www.altpress.com/suicideboys-sing-me-a-lullaby-my-sweet-temptation-interview/.

Juice WRLD and the Question of the Archive

1 Laura McInnes, "Long Live Juice WRLD: The 2018 Lost Interview," Sniffers, July 16, 2020. https://www.sniffers.co.nz/article/juice-wrld-long-lost-2018-interview

2 Eric Isom, "It's All Authentic: An Interview With Juice WRLD," *Complex*, April 16, 2018. https://www.complex.com/pigeons-and-planes/2018/04/juice-wrld-interview.

3 "Juice WRLD's First Radio Interview with Lil Bibby [2018]," *Power92Chicago*, December 9, 2019. Video, 13:20, https://www.youtube.com/watch?v=CNtyetNfHYM.

4 Tom Connick, "Juice WRLD: the emo rapper on his surprise hit 'Lucid Dreams,'" *NME*, September 18, 2018. https://www.nme.com/blogs/nme-blogs/juice-wrld-interview-lucid-dreams-2374917.

5 Dan Hyman, "The Life and Death of Juice WRLD," *GQ*, May 3, 2021. https://www.gq.com/story/the-life-and-death-of-juice-wrld.

6 Sheldon Pearce, "Juice WRLD: 'All Girls Are the Same' Track Review," *Pitchfork*, March 5, 2018. https://pitchfork.com/reviews/tracks/juice-wrld-all-girls-are-the-same/.

7 "How G Herbo Embraced His 'Swervo' Side to Paint a Full Picture of Chicago," *DJBooth*, August 1, 2018. https://djbooth.net/features/2018-08-01-g-herbo-swervo-interview.

8 Carrie Battan, "Lil Xan and the Year in Sad Rap," *The New Yorker*, January 1, 2018. https://www.newyorker.com/magazine/2018/01/08/lil-xan-and-the-year-in-sad-rap.

9 Tajah Ware, "An Interview with Juice Wrld," *Elevator*, September 20, 2017. https://web.archive.org/web/20180416143413/http://www.elevatormag.com/juicewrld-interview.

10 Rebecca Schiller, "Juice WRLD on Writing 'Lucid Dreams': He Breaks It Down in New Interview," *Billboard*, July 10, 2018. https://www.billboard.com/music/rb-hip-hop/juice-wrld-writing-lucid-dreams-interview-8464428/.

11 "Juice WRLD on Creating His Smash Hit 'Lucid Dreams': 'It Was Nothing Special,'" *DJBooth*, February 13, 2019. https://djbooth.net/features/2019-02-13-juice-wrld-lucid-dreams-nothing-special-hit.